HENRY NAYLOR

Henry Naylor is a British comedy writer, producer, director and performer, best known for his award-winning writing, and for working with comedy partner Andy Parsons in *Parsons and Naylor's Pull-Out Sections*. He was a lead writer for *Spitting Image*, and has written for many well-known award-winning British TV and radio shows including *Alas Smith and Jones*, *Dead Ringers* and *Alistair McGowan's Big Impression*.

The Collector marked a departure from comedy for Henry. It was first presented at the Gilded Balloon at the 2014 Edinburgh Fringe to great critical acclaim and won a Scotsman Fringe First Award for Outstanding Writing. Forming the first instalment in the *Arabian Nightmares* trilogy of plays, *The Collector* then had a sell-out run at London's Arcola Theatre in November 2014.

Echoes followed, opening at the Gilded Balloon, Edinburgh, in August 2015. After winning the Spirit of the Fringe Award, the play transferred both to the Arcola Theatre in London, and to the 59E59 Theater off-Broadway in New York. At the 2016 Adelaide Fringe Festival, *Echoes* became one of the most decorated shows at the festival's history, winning five major Fringe Awards, including Best Theatre.

Henry's most recent work, and final part of the trilogy, *Angel*, premiered at the 2016 Edinburgh Festival Fringe, winning two major awards, including another Scotsman Fringe First. In December, *The Times* named *Angel* as one of the Ten Best Plays of 2016.

Other Titles in this Series

Henry Naylor

ARABIAN NIGHTMARES

The Collector
Echoes
Angel

NICK HERN BOOKS

London
www.nickhernbooks.co.uk

A Nick Hern Book

Arabian Nightmares first published in Great Britain in 2017 as a paperback original by Nick Hern Books Limited, The Glasshouse, 49a Goldhawk Road, London W12 8QP

Arabian Nightmares copyright © 2017 Henry Naylor

Henry Naylor has asserted his moral right to be identified as the author of these plays

Cover photograph by Rosalind Furlong, with Filipa Bragança as the Angel

Designed and typeset by Nick Hern Books, London
Printed in the UK by Mimeo Ltd, Huntingdon, Cambridgeshire PE29 6XX

A CIP catalogue record for this book is available from the British Library

ISBN 978 1 84842 634 4

Woodland CARBON
www.woodlandcarbon.co.uk
NICK HERN BOOKS
Printed on Carbon Captured paper

A Few Thank-Yous

First, thanks to Anne Naylor, Deb and Phil – without whom no art would get made! Massive thanks to the Korens: Karen Koren, Katy Koren and Kristian Koren – and Paul Sullivan – all friends as well as co-workers. Love to the wonderful staff at the Gilded Balloon, including Rowan, Lyndsey, Steph, David, Richard, Molly and Daniel. The Arcola team, including Mehmet and Leyla. In Adelaide, Martha Lott and her top gang at Holden Street, including Tracey Mathers; Neil Ward and Angela Tolley, top Aussie publicists, my buddies Heather Croall and Nick Phillips, Michelle Buxton, David Grybowski and Lizzie Hines. In New York, the 59E59 gang, especially Elysabeth and Peter. In Prague, Steve Gove and his posse. To Sam Maynard, I owe a huge thanks, for helping me start on this path. Danny Dougramachi has been great helping me research. The fab directors Michael Cabot and Emma Buttler; the lighting designers Ross Bibby and Andy Grange, the many technicians we've worked with, including Alia Stephens, Sofia, Sholto, Holly Curtis and Eric Morel. A massive shout-out to Kathryn Cabot and Kathryn Barker prods for doing a fab tour of *The Collector*. Sean Gascoine, Amy Sparks, Nicki Stoddart, Hannah Begbie, Kitty Laing, Maureen Vincent and Carly Peters of United Agents – not just top agents, but lovely people. Huge thanks to Sarah Liisa Wilkinson, Matt Applewhite and Jodi Gray of Nick Hern Books. Not forgetting the magnificent Rosalind Furlong, Steve Ullathorne and Alan Moyle for some stellar photos. Viv and Leo, obviously. And Phil Goodwin, who's helped me enormously at various stages. Then there's the magnificent casts of the three shows – Filipa, Felicity, William, Lesley, Ritu, Rachel, Shireen and Olivia – honoured to have worked with you. Finally, my wonderful, hilarious, beautiful, uber-smart wife Sarah, who has to put up with me when I'm writing! – Love you, love you all.

The photograph of Filipa Bragança as the Angel, taken by Rosalind Furlong, on the front cover was kindly reproduced with the permission of the Bragança family. Filipa was a great friend and inspiration, and the picture is included as a tribute and mark of respect for her performances in both *Echoes* and *Angel*.

THE COLLECTOR

The Collector was first performed at the Gilded Balloon, Edinburgh, on 30 July 2014, with the following cast:

ZOYA/THE NARRATOR	Ritu Arya
KASPER	William Reay
FOSTER	Lesley Harcourt
Director	Henry Naylor

It was produced by Henry Naylor and the Gilded Balloon's Karen Koren.

The show transferred to the Arcola Theatre, London, in November 2014, restaged by director Michael Cabot, and with lighting design by Ross Bibby.

Kathryn Barker Productions under the auspices of Kathryn Cabot launched their own tour of the show in autumn 2016, with the following cast:

ZOYA/THE NARRATOR	Shireen Farkhoy
KASPER	William Reay
FOSTER	Olivia Beardsley
Director	Michael Cabot
Lighting Designer	Andy Grange
Stage Manager	Holly Curtis

To SLK
For everything xx

Characters

ZOYA, *an Iraqi woman*
KASPER, *an American reservist, forties*
FOSTER, *an American interrogator, twenty-four*

The story of The Collector *is told by three different storytellers.*
They each speak directly to the audience, through the 'fourth
wall'.

First to speak, a young, beautiful Iraqi woman, ZOYA. *She's*
strong, smart – a modern Scheherazade. She begins her
narration like it's the start of The Arabian Nights...

ZOYA   Here is the land of magic and genies and
        flying carpets.
        Of tyrants and despots and murderous Ba'athists.
        A land of sweetmeats and Turkish delights,
        Of Sinbad and Saddam and Arabian Nights.
        It's a magical nation of fable and mystery
        A place with a long and ancient history
        Boasting a rich and combustible soil,
        Fertilised with blood and soaked in oil.
        Writing began here and even drawing,
        And beating with hoses and waterboarding.
        Ours is the story of all mankind
        Of the triumphs and failings of the human mind.
        So if you're with us, or against us, pull up
        your chairs
        And share with us these Arabian nightmares.

        COLONEL 'KASPER' KASPROWICZ. *He's*
        a charismatic American reservist. Mid-forties.
        The head honcho at Mazrat Prison.

KASPER No one liked going into cell C27, after the Nassir
        incident. Not even the dogs.
        Full of bad spirits.
        But I didn't believe in ghosts. Used to say I'll
        believe in 'em when I see 'em.
        Then came 17th December 2003. The day after
        'Nassir'.
        We had a prisoner we called 'Tom Selleck' – cos
        he looked like Tom Selleck – who launched a dirty

protest. Imagine Magnum PI smearing his cell in shit.

We had to punish the guy, hard.

But what could we do? We kicked his ass every night already. We needed a punishment to match the severity of the crime.

So I thought 'Let's fuck him up; let's put him in C27.'

So we dragged him in.

And to begin with he was just crying and complaining…

Nothing out of the ordinary.

And we settled in to play cards in the guards' room.

…Six o'clock, nothing. Seven o'clock – nothing. Eight o'clock… he starts screaming.

Proper screaming. Tried to ignore it.

…But then we heard, The Thud.

The sound of a body falling heavily on the floor. Over and over.

Thud. Thud. Thud.

Fuck. I mean fuck.

Don't care what Tom Selleck had done. Couldn't leave him there.

So we're running up the stairs, shouting and hollering, trying to drown out our fears… when the noises… the screaming, the thuds.. suddenly stop.

And I get to the cell. And Selleck's crouching in the corner. And he's whimpering.

And I look across. And he's not alone.

There's a figure standing there.

Dressed in black.

Silent.

Unmoving. And it has no face. Just a soul-sucking dark shadow where a face should be.

When people talk about ghosts – they say they feel a presence. Not me. I felt the absence. The despair of the void.

And for the first time that war, I was scared.

*A transition; we've moved back in time, to the
start of the story.*

ZOYA   Under Saddam, there was one popular music
station – controlled by his son, Uday: 'The Voice
of Youth.'
Played our leading boy band – Unknown to No
One – on loop.
Their biggest hit? A song honouring Saddam's
birthday, which was played twice an hour.
'Get up, get up, let me hear you say,
To the Father of the People: Happy Birthday.'
Or some such thing.
Crazy.
Would be like NSYNC singing George Dubya
their compliments of the season.
Just occasionally, 'The Voice' played Boyzone.
But as war loomed, even they got banned. In Iraq,
even Ronan Keating was dangerous and edgy.'

So, you can imagine: Western music was all
underground, performed in deserted garages,
sweaty backrooms…

That was I how I first saw Nassir. He was singing
Eminem covers in a defunct warehouse.
Shaved head, telling everybody he was Slim
Shady, the Real Slim Shady.
Was subversive.
Rebellious.
Very rebellious; it was dangerous to play Western
music in the weeks before the war. Showed a
'troubling affinity' with the enemy.
So we, Nassir and his crowd, were risking a lot for
his art…
But it was worth it.
For me.
I fell in love with him at first sight.
He was selling CDs after his gig. I had to have
one. If only to be able to talk to him.
'You're risking a lot. Aren't you worried about the
Mukhabarat?' I asked him.

'The secret police? They'd put you in prison for owning a Westlife CD.'

'Maybe they don't get everything wrong.'

He laughed, a warm smile. 'You love music? Proper music?'

'I'm a collector. Eminem, Tupac.'

'Heard any Ludacris?'

And he gave me a Ludacris CD.

Most people fall in love to 'love songs'. But not us. 'Our song' was 'Pimpin' All Over the World'.

Didn't take us long to start talking of marriage. But my father, he was opposed.

'He is a musician. Musicians never have money.' And annoyingly, he was right. Nassir spent all his money on CDs. We always used to joke, that if you gave him a dollar, he'd swap it for Fiddy Cents.

'I won't let my eldest daughter live in poverty.'

Nassir of course, tried to laugh it off.

'What do we do?' I said.

'There's only one thing we can do. In the words of Fiddy, we got to get rich. Or die trying.'

FOSTER, *a smart, spirited, twenty-four-year-old American interrogator – knows what she wants.*

FOSTER   At Camp Huachuca, I learned the German philosophy of interrogation. The Germans believed that violence produces bad intel; it's proven, scientifically, that prisoners will say anything to stop the pain. Better to tease out confessions using psychological tricks.

I'll give you an example from my own experience.

Once had this prisoner – who nobody could break down. All the interrogators had had a go. And I was determined to be the one, who broke him. So I was up all the night before, preparing and preparing hundreds of questions. Fear Ups, and Fear Downs, Pride and Ego Downs, Rapid-fires – basically all the techniques.

But when I sat in the booth, and was faced with
the actual physical presence of the prisoner, the
questions all seemed irrelevant.
His body language was closed. He was nervous,
shaking, keyed up. Ready for verbal resistance and
a fight.
And so I ditched my strategy; did the last thing he
was expecting.
I said nothing.
And the prisoner couldn't handle it. Started
shuffling uncomfortably. Was expecting the usual
Alpha-Male battle-of-wills.
Instead of which, he was faced with a woman.
Staring at him. Saying nothing.

And after a couple of minutes of silence he started
to babble. To fill the vacuum.

After an hour: he'd told me everything.
I'd said nothing; he'd interrogated himself.

And it works. You can make anyone reveal their
true self – you just have to find the right trigger.

ZOYA   After the Americans came, it wasn't just the
musicians who were poor. All Saddam's men were
fired, without pay: bureaucrats, soldiers,
policemen – loitering on the streets.
Everyone seemed destined to 'die tryin''.

My father began desperately trying to find me
a husband, 'a man of means'.

One day he said, 'I found you a Wealthy Man,
with prospects' – a smuggler, an ex-police officer,
who now traded in arms.
'But,' said my father, 'he likes music, and he looks
like a film star.'
When we met, I was shocked. The closest 'film
star' he resembled was Freddy Krueger. He was a
brutish Mukhabarat with a scar-face. Called Faisal.
He leered as we met. 'Your father says you collect
music. I collect music, too.'

'Ah, like what?'

'Like Unknown to No One. "Get up, get up, Let me hear you say, To the Father of the People: Happy Birthday."'

'My preferences are a bit more hardcore than that,' I told him coldly.

'Ah. Ronan Keating,' he nodded sagely.

I fled downtown, leaving Faisal angry, bitter, rejected.

I secretly met Nassir in the queue for a gas bottle. We held hands, and laughed about the man with the scar.
Singing Ronan Keating's 'hardcore' 'When You Say Nothing At All' in the style of Dr Dre.

KASPER   We were a unit of reservists. Brought in to maintain the peace.
            With useful skills. We were doctors, carpenters, insurance clerks, fishermen. But none of us had run a prison.

            I told my superiors that I didn't have the expertise, but they didn't want to know.
            Just said, 'Captain, we have an insurgency to deal with. If you can't handle this, we will find someone who can... *Can* you handle it, Captain?'
            'Yes, sir, I can handle it, sir.'

            So I took over Mazrat Jail.
            Used to be one of Saddam's most notorious prisons.
            They say ten thousand people died there.
            Was bad, real bad. When we arrived, there were still butcher's hooks in the ceiling.

FOSTER   Chairs with straps.

KASPER   Bloodstains.

FOSTER   A room with a trapdoor.

KASPER   Some of the grunts freaked out. Complained of bad karma. Said we should bulldoze the place. Me...? I saw an opportunity. What better way to

show the righteousness of our cause? – than to
convert this hellhole – into a model prison.
So I ordered the grunts to put out washcloths,
towels, toothpaste, prayer mats.

But not all of them understood what we were
doing. They weren't trained. They were combat
officers not prison guards. Not what you'd call
'enlightened'.

One of them, a loudmouth called Vallay says:
'Why are we doing this, giving them washcloths
and shit, sir? These are prisoners?'
I told him: 'We're doing this because we have an
obligation. We're doing this to help others
experience the freedoms that WE take for granted.
We're doing this because we're from the most
blessed nation on earth.'
Vallay laughed. 'Bullshit. I'm doin' this to blow
shit up.'

So I said, 'Come with me.'
And took Vallay to the gates, where were there
were four Iraqis waiting. Each had an arm missing.
I asked the Iraqis, 'Why you here?'
And they showed us their stumps.
Told us when they were imprisoned here, Saddam
cut their arms off. For punishment. And they'd
come to collect them, cos they thought they knew
where they were buried.
…I turned to Vallay, said, 'That's why we're here,
son. *That's* why we're here.'

FOSTER   When I was posted to Mazrat, I was really excited.
This was my chance to test my skills against
REAL Bad Guys in a REAL warzone.
Couldn't wait.
There were six of us from Camp Huachuca. Ready
to break the insurgency.
Soon as we arrived at Mazrat, the other five were
all assigned prisoners for interrogation.
But me? – nothing.

I went to see the logistics officer. He was about
fifty, a snuffing-shrew of a man, called Staff
Sergeant Dunning.

I said, 'Sir, I'm ready to commence interrogations,
sir.'

But he said, 'You just rest, Sergeant Foster.'

And I'm confused, I'm... None of the others had
been asked to rest, just me.

'Sir, I don't need to rest, sir. I'm ready to start, sir.'

Wouldn't look me in the eyes, just pretended to
read paperwork, muttering, 'That's an order,
Sergeant Foster.'

So I wait for an explanation.

But – nothing. His body language? – closed.

And suddenly it made sense.

'...Is this cos I'm a woman, sir?'

And that's when he snaps. 'Women are too soft,
too compassionate for a combat zone. Lack the
necessary – '

' – Sir, I came top in my year at Camp
Huachuca, sir.'

'Is that supposed to impress me, Sergeant? This
ain't no college exercise. This is a real combat
zone. And whilst the head honchos are playing
their games with sexual politics, American boys
are being killed.'

So I went to see Captain Kasprowicz.

KASPER   First time I met Sergeant Foster, she bursts into
my office. Yelling and cussing. Saying: 'I thought
we were trying to bring Freedom to this country?'

So I listen, and listen.

And when she finishes...

I summon Staff Sergeant Dunning. And say:

'Dunning? We are at war. The enemy, here, is the
insurgent. Does *she* look like an insurgent?'

'No, sir.'

'Do you know what she looks like to me?'

'A woman, sir?'

'A passionate, dedicated soldier who represents
the best traditions of the US Military.'

'Yessir.'

'Now do your job, and let Sergeant Foster do hers.'

FOSTER   Captain Kasprowicz had my back from the start.
I liked that… We were going to get on just fine…
Dunning wasn't the biggest pain in the ass. That
was Vallay.

I'd been taught that 'brutality was unnecessary' to
get good intel.

Vallay had gotten all his ideas about interrogation
from watching Jack Bauer in *24*. He couldn't
understand why I wasn't using pliers and
blowtorches.

One day, Vallay was on guard, and I was
interrogating a General using the Pride and Ego
Down technique.

The General had been refusing to talk, insisting on
being interrogated by a Senior Officer.

I hoped that if I offended his pride and ego enough,
he'd big himself up, boast about his achievements.
 So I kept calling him 'Sergeant'.

'Sergeant??' he bellowed. 'Don't you know who
I am? I am a General, I sat at the right-hand side
of Saddam, you fucking little whore.'

He'd taken the bait, was just beginning to talk
when suddenly WHAM;

Vallay punched him clean off his chair.

Unprompted. Yelling 'Don't you call the lady
a whore, you fucking piece of shit.'

I'm up and 'What the fuck, Vallay? WHAT. THE.
FUCK?'

'He calls you a whore, you should stand up for
yourself, ma'am. Show him who won the war,
ma'am.'

'HE WAS TELLING ME WHAT HE DID FOR
SADDAM, YOU MORON.'

I helped the General up. He was bleeding and
angry.

The interrogation was over.

The General clammed up. The rest of the session
became about him not giving in to Vallay.

Everything appeared to be peaceful. But
underneath, the battlelines were being drawn for a
new kind of conflict.
These foes weren't the forces of insurgency or the
forces of America. But the forces of
Enlightenment and Darkness.

ZOYA   A chance encounter changed everything.
Nassir, passing through a checkpoint, heard the
American soldiers playing Metallica.
Asked if he could buy the CD.
Now, the soldiers were bemused. Because Nassir
didn't speak textbook American.
He was self-taught, from his hip-hop collection.
He said, 'How much for your motherfucking
CD, dog?'

Made them laugh so much, they *gave* him the CD.
And that's how it started.

He went every day to the checkpoint. And every
day they burned him a new disc.
Soon, he was teasing them, joking about the lack
of electricity.
Telling them: 'How come you can put a man on
the moon. But you can't put a man on an electric
substation?'
And they laughed, and laughed.

Till one day, they said, 'Hey, dog, we could use
you…'

Nassir comes to find me. Excited. Says to me, 'We
"got rich". I found a job. Pays $660 a month.
Enough for your father?'
'Er, yes… Stupid question.' Three times more than
a teacher. 'What is this job?'
'A translator for the Americans.'
'No,' I said, 'no. It is dangerous. The Insurgents – '
Nassir laughed. 'The Insurgents will lose.
The Americans are good people. We must give
them time.'

'How much time?'

'They'll have sorted this all out in a couple of months. You just see. By 2004 – there'll be democracy. Right across the region, from Algeria to Yemen. Mark my words.'

Mark my words…

And so he took a job for the Americans.

FOSTER   So I was given this new translator:
Nassir.
Was cool. Handsome.
Liked America, loved music.

First time Nassir and I worked together, I was monstering a prisoner. Yelling in his face.
Nassir just watched. Puzzled.
The louder I yelled, the softer Nassir talked.
Till I could hardly hear him.
Suddenly Nassir says, 'Why are you shouting? Iraqi people don't shout. It is against our principles.'
I said, 'I'm intimidating the prisoner.'
And he laughs. He says, 'You won't intimidate anyone. These people are used to Saddam.'
And I think about the chair with the straps, and the room with the trapdoor, and I know he's right. So I say, 'Okay. What would you do?'
He says, 'Get me some Oreos, some Cheese Doodles and some Twinkies.'
Seems a bit weird, but I give him what he wants.
Then he says to the prisoner, 'You are Sunni, yes? Listen. If you don't answer her questions, she'll just transfer you to the Government. The *Shia* Government. How do you think *they* will treat you?'
Two minutes later, the prisoner's told us everything.
Fabulous. This guy's a keeper.
…But I say – 'What were the Oreos, the Cheese Doodles and the Twinkies for?'
And he says, 'Oh. They were for me.'

…Good translators don't just translate words.
Good translators also convey Spirit and Ideals.

Good translators don't just take Iraqi and make
it American; good translators take Iraq and make
it America.

Nassir was a good translator.

ZOYA   I'd had a bad day.
Someone had syphoned my petrol.
I suspected my neighbours.
They'd shown a lot of jealousy, particularly about
Nassir. He was good-looking, eligible. And he was
Employed.
The neighbours often made snide comments about
his job. Because he was not only bringing home
$660 a month – but also unlimited supplies of
Cheese Doodles.
Sadly he didn't bring home any petrol. I queued at
the garage from 6.30 a.m. till 2 – at which point
the petrol ran out.
I'd wasted a day, came home dusty and furious.
To find my father, Nassir's parents, and Nassir.
Standing there grinning. Holding armfuls of Oreos
and Twinkies.
'What are you doing?'
'We're having a party,' said Nassir.
'Why?'
'Your father said "yes".'
I laughed. 'What – we're getting married? Fine.
But we're not inviting the neighbours.'
Happy times.

FOSTER Nassir and I were a great team, getting intel faster
than ever.
He was becoming real popular round camp. He
monopolised the karaoke CD in the Mortar Café.
Rapping to Dr Dre's 'Next Episode'.
His voice was great; he admitted to being
a musician.
So we asked to hear his stuff.
But he was shy.
'You are from America. The home of music. You
won't like it.'

'Put it on,' we said.
After a lot of persuasion, he put one of his CDs.
We're all relieved. We liked it.
Nassir was ecstatic. Told us his dream was to drive
around America, and play his music in the great
musical cities.
The brother of one of the guards runs a bar in
Nashville. Tells him when the war is over, he'll
get him a gig.
I never saw Nassir happier.
These were the good times.

ZOYA   The happy times...

KASPER   The good times...

          Lighting change to indicate a change in mood.

          Everything changed Tuesday November 25, 2003.
          Was Eid. The day they break the fast of Ramadan.
          Everybody was celebrating. On the street. Visiting
          their families.

FOSTER   Nassir had brought me some leftovers. Sweet rice
          with raisins. Some cold, grilled chicken.
          Delicious, when all you've been eating is MREs.

KASPER   Then, the explosion.
          Although it was five miles away, we knew it
          was bad.

FOSTER   Almost instantly, a huge grey twist of smoke.

KASPER   Sirens. The helicopters.

FOSTER   A bomb in the market.

KASPER   One hundred and twenty-seven dead.
          Who was the perp? The patrols don't know. They
          sweep up everybody in the vicinity. And I mean
          EVERYBODY. Kids. Old women. Beggars.
          Shoppers.

FOSTER   They felt the bad guys would be among them
          SOMEWHERE. And it was up to us to find them.

KASPER   I want to make some releases.
           'Permission denied.'
           No one wants to be responsible for freeing
           a terrorist.

FOSTER   So we end up working round the clock. Stupid
           hours. Twenty-hour shifts – just to get through
           the backlog.
           We're dead on our feet. About to take a break.
           When a big guy is brought into the booth. A mean
           fucker. Scar across his face.
           And Nassir goes white.
           'I know this man. They call him Faisal. He was
           high up in the Mukhabarat.'
           …Suddenly Faisal hisses something.
           Nassir doesn't translate.
           'What did he say?' I ask.
           And Nassir replies: 'He says "You are dead".'
           Then Faisal says in English, 'I didn't mean you,
           lady.' He turns to Nassir. 'I meant you,
           collaborator. You, YOU are dead.'
           'Don't worry,' I tell Nassir. 'He's going nowhere.'

ZOYA   Faisal, brutal Faisal.
           'It's alright,' he said. 'He can't do anything,' he
           said. 'He's locked up, forever,' he said.
           He said.

KASPER   Next morning.
           The exercise yard is crammed with people, most
           of them innocent.
           One of the detainees strides to the fence. Shouts at
           the watchtower, his arm around his boy –
           'When are you going to let us go? We haven't
           done anything…'
           The sentry in the watchtower ignores the prisoner.
           'At least let my boy go. Do you think he is
           a terrorist? Him?? Do you think he's Al-Qaeda??'
           A crowd begins to form. 'Yeah, yeah, let him go.'
           The sentry should have told them to move back
           right there. Right then. He didn't.

The crowd grows.
The prisoner they called Faisal, suddenly chants:
'Bora bedan nefdeike ya Saddam!' – 'Our blood,
our souls, are yours, oh Saddam.'
One prisoner joins in. Two. Five.
'Bora bedan nefdeike ya Saddam!'
All the crowd take the chant. Three, four hundred
prisoners.
Swarming towards the tower. *'Bora bedan
nefdeike ya Saddam!'*
Now the sentry shouts into his megaphone. 'Move
back fifty feet. I said move back.'
Too late. No one can hear him.
Suddenly BOOM! BOOM! BOOM!
Mortars. From outside. The prison under fire.
Surely a coordinated attack.
Chaos. Dust grit.
BOOM!
A section of the prison wall falls.
BOOM!
Shouting screaming firing falling. Prisoners
swarming, scrabbling through dust clouds and
pain. Reaching the hole, scrambling through.
One of the escapees was Faisal.

ZOYA From then on – I lived in fear.
Faisal had escaped. Faisal wanted Nassir dead.
I was scared for us.
'Calm, calm, calm,' Nassir told me. 'Don't worry be
happy. Be strong. The Americans will protect us.'
Calm, he said.
He said.

Nassir had a friend called Zaheer.
He was a translator too.
Nassir always used to have lunch with him at
the base.
He was an English teacher, a gentle man. Loved
Shakespeare.
So much so that Nassir said his translations were
in iambic pentameter.

One day, Zaheer didn't turn up for work. No explanation.

Sometimes translators quit. Didn't want to be seen as collaborators.

Family pressure.

But that didn't fit. Nassir thought he would have said SOMETHING.

Anyhow. A couple of days later.

Zaheer's car was found, downtown.

Flat tyres.

The door torn off.

Completely abandoned. Zaheer himself – nowhere to be seen.

Vanished without leaving a note. Without telling anyone. Not even his family.

Nassir said he wasn't worried.

But suddenly he started bringing me gifts.

Bringing me Western clothes, LOTS of Western clothes.

It's important for him that I wear them. Apparently they're a statement.

'I don't care about the clothes,' I told him. 'Don't get killed; don't be a martyr. Quit.'

'No,' he said. 'No. If people like us give in, there is no hope for this country. This is about building a new future.'

But the more things he bought me, the more I saw doubt in his face.

KASPER   After the attack on the prison, there were sudden changes.

Mazrat was officially a hotbed of the insurgency. My jail was the frontline.

Even the OGA – the Other Government Agency – wanted a base here.

They took over one of our buildings. The OGA! A big deal. I'm pumped, I'm psyched.

We'd get more high-profile prisoners: guys from the deck of cards.

FOSTER   Captain Kasper: sweet, naive Kasper.
I liked his passion, but never shared it.
I knew WE wouldn't get any of the high-level
detainees. I knew it.
The OGA – the Other Government Agency would
take them all.
The one consolation: I wouldn't be working with
Vallay any more.
The OGA wanted him.
Wanted him to 'prepare their prisoners for
interrogation'.
I walked past Vallay on the parade ground.
He was walking with a swagger, now.
'Yo, Foster,' he taunts, 'I'm gonna get the Four
of Clubs.'
'What in hell?' I told him. 'Why do YOU get HIM?'
'Because your approach is old-fashioned. Your
interrogation techniques belong to the Cold War.
We're dealing with a new kind of enemy.'
'Is that what the OGA told you?'
He just smirked, and left singing 'America the
Free'.

ZOYA   I'm wearing my new clothes down the market.
They're a political statement. A declaration of my
affinity with the West.
I see the usual stalls selling colourful spices; stalls
selling tomatoes; belts. Then the new stalls
reaching out to a new market. The stalls selling
CDs of Sadr's sermons. The stalls selling DVDs
of American convoys being blown-up. Of
collaborators being beheaded.
One of the DVDs has Zaheer's photo on its sleeve.
It's an execution video.
I feel sick. I'm about to leave when one of my
neighbours grabs my arm. She's a shrivelled
woman with a sour face. She sneers, 'Did your
collaborator boyfriend buy you these clothes?'
I'm still reeling from seeing Zaheer.
'My "collaborator boyfriend" is working for
a better Iraq – for everyone.'

She calls me a whore.
I snatch the Zaheer video off the stall, and thrust it
in her face. 'Is that what you want for your
country? Are these the people you want to rule us?'
A crowd is forming. A hostile crowd.
I push through.
The crone waves a DVD of the UN bombing
after me:
'Run, run. The Americans won't protect you. They
can't even protect their own.'

Nassir visits that night.
'Why aren't you wearing your new clothes?'
He asks me. 'You mustn't hide away. If we want
freedom for this country, we have to stand up for
what we believe.'
'I burned them,' I confess.
'Burned them??'
'...Zaheer was filmed with a death squad. Zaheer
was beheaded.'

Nassir says nothing.

FOSTER   About this time, Nassir suddenly started coming in
to the booth in a balaclava.
'Ho,' I said. '– what are you wearing that for?
You look like a terrorist.'
'I don't want people knowing who I am.'
'Come on, you should be proud. You're creating
a free Iraq, you should be celebrating it.'
But he doesn't take it off.

I go into the Mortar Café one night after a long shift.
Grab a nasty cup of coffee.
There's more people here than usual.
A lot of strangers, listening to some guy's stories...
It's Vallay...
One guy's flicking through photos on a camera.
Laughing. 'This is fucked up, man.'
'It's the OGA. It's how we roll,' laughs Vallay.
I join the throng. Look through the shoulders.
'What the hell?' I gasp. 'Vallay? Is that a picture
of a prisoner in a dress?? Why would you do that?'

Vallay sneers: 'State-of-the-art interrogation.
We're fucking with the Arab psyche.'
'By playing dress-ups?'
'If you humiliate 'em they're more ready to talk.'
I grab the camera. Flick through the images.
Prisoners in dresses. Prisoners in crucifixion
poses. Piles of naked prisoners. Prisoners being
forced to masturbate.

KASPER   Foster came to see me.
With a camera. Vallay's camera.
Said, 'You need to know what's going on in your
camp.' Said: 'This has got to be illegal.'
And she showed me the pictures.

What could I say?
Was shocked. Horrified.
Said, 'What do you want *me* to do? Geneva
doesn't apply. Ours aren't "Prisoners of War" –
they're "security detainees". They can do this.'

When she'd gone I consulted the rules.
There were five different versions. All contradicting
each other.
In one, Stress Positions were allowed. In another
they were banned. Then dogs were permitted,
outlawed, permitted again...
There were so many rules, there were no rules.
It was chaos. You could argue a case for almost
anything...

*A change in lighting, to indicate a break from
the action.*

FOSTER   Forty-two years ago, at Stanford University,
a psychologist called Zimbardo launched an
experiment, investigating how situation and
environment can override morality. The idea was
simple – take a group of student-volunteers, tell
half of them they are prisoners, the other half
prison wardens, place them in a makeshift jail and
let them make up their own rules.
The experiment was meant to last two weeks but
was ended abruptly just six days later, after an

outbreak of sadism. Student guards began
stripping the student prisoners naked, putting bags
over their heads, depriving them of sleep and
humiliating them sexually.

This is what humans do.
This is who we are.

Lights change; back to the action again.

ZOYA   One afternoon, at prayers, my father goes to the
local mosque. He takes his shoes off, walks inside.
Then sees a poster. And the poster has Nassir's
face on it. Smiling.

That night, my father confronts Nassir – shows
him the poster.
'You are on a blacklist. There are death lists all
over town. They show your name, address, phone
number. They even got your picture.'
Nassir sees the picture, says: 'This IS terrible…
I got red-eye from the flash.'
But no one laughs.
'If you love your family, you will stop working for
the Americans.'

When no one was looking, I saw the fear beneath
Nassir's mask.

KASPER   Nassir comes to me next morning. Frightened.
Demanding Asylum – for his fiancée and himself.
Right there, right then.
I take him to the Asylum Officer, say:
'Can we fast-track this applicant, it's an urgent
case.'
'Sir. There are procedures.'
'With all due respect, there are people who will
kill this man the minute he leaves this base.'
'After 9/11 there are strict screens on Iraqi
citizens – '
' – this man has laid his life on the line for
America.'
'Sir, we're fighting a war, that's our priority right
now. We can't go faster.'

There was nothing to be done, nothing to be said.
We left.

Nassir was quiet. Very quiet.

FOSTER   My two o'clock interrogation came. No Nassir.
Waited till two-thirty. Still none.
Asked around.
'Where's Nassir?'
Only the guys on the gates had seen him. 'Left
couple of hours ago. Said he was quitting.'
Quitting.

Shameful.
The best translator we had. A true friend of
America. Had quit.

KASPER   She comes to me, she's angry, sharp, but cold.
Tells me Nassir would be impossible to replace.

FOSTER   Tell him, 'If somebody works for you, loyally,
putting their life on the line – it's our duty to
protect them.'

KASPER   What could I say? I can't change the policy of the
US Government Asylum Office?? So I told her I
thought the Asylum Office were doing a great job.

FOSTER   He didn't believe that shit about the Asylum
Office; his body language screamed LIE.

KASPER   Told her I wasn't lying, and I rubbed my nose.

FOSTER   Told him it's my job to know when people are
lying, and when they're lying, they rub their nose.

KASPER   Told her I wasn't lying, and I covered my mouth.

FOSTER   Said it's my job to know when people are lying,
and when they're lying they cover their mouth.

KASPER   Told her, emphatically, I wasn't lying – and I look
to the left.

FOSTER   Said emphatically, when people are lying – they
look to the l… Then I started laughing.

KASPER   And when I sat on my hands – she got hysterical.

FOSTER   He wasn't a good liar.

KASPER   We got talking. She told me about body language.
Told her I wished I could have read body language
when I was a kid. Would have made it easier to
find who was attracted to me at high school.

FOSTER   We got talking. He wanted to know what the
telltale signs of sexual attraction were.
I said a 'bulge in the trousers'.
We laughed. And that's when I noticed the bulge
in his.

KASPER   …What happened shouldn't have happened. But
in the war zone. People do stupid things. They're
desperate for human contact. To feel the life force.

FOSTER   It was a mistake. Senior Officers aren't supposed
to sleep with Juniors. If the wrong person saw…
could spell trouble.
Which is ultimately what happened.
Someone opened the door. They saw us.
They saw.
Who was it? We didn't know. But right then, we
didn't care.

ZOYA   That evening, when Nassir drives home, it's dark.
He's tired, desperate for bed, and nearly misses
the car outside his house. Until a small flame
lights the interior.
A cigarette.
There are four men inside…
Heart thumping, Nassir drives on.

An hour later, my sister wakes me. 'Your
boyfriend's here. He's waiting in the lounge.'
'What time is it?' I say.
'After midnight,' she replies.
'Why are you here now?'
He has tears in his eyes.
'What's wrong?'
'I don't know where to go. There was a car full of
Faisal's people outside my place. I'm moving

from house to house. I got nowhere to stay.'
'It's okay, it's okay. You can stay here tonight.'

Three o'clock in the morning, BANG BANG on
the door.
I snap awake.
BANG BANG BANG.
'Coming.'
I rush Nassir into the women's quarters.
My mother, my sisters – confused, half-asleep.
Suddenly wide awake, shocked, horrified by the
presence of a man.
I motion for them to be quiet.
BANG BANG BANG.
'Coming coming coming.'
My father gets to the door first.
Faisal and three men force their way in.
'Where is he? We know he's here.'
'Know WHO'S here?'
'Nassir.'
My father, unaware of Nassir's presence, is
convincing when he said, 'There's no Nassir here.
Come and have a look.'
They come in. Smash chairs, bang doors. Look in
rooms, in cupboards – everywhere except the
women's quarters.
'Okay, look in there,' says Faisal.
My mother blocks the doorway, fierce. 'Shame on
you. Shame. You would enter the women's
quarters!?! Shame. There are no men in there.
What do you think we are?'
Faisal's men pause. Look at him for guidance.
He nods grimly.
As they leave – 'We're watching you.'

Nassir could sleep on the sofa for one night.
'Thank you, Father.'

I was awake long after the house fell silent.
Crept into the lounge. Found Nassir the colour of
metal in the moonlight.
…We tried to cram a life's worth of experience
into a night.

'Don't die,' I told him. 'Don't die. Don't let them take you. I love you I love you.'

At daybreak he was gone.

KASPER   Unexpectedly, Nassir returned to us.
Entering the base, he was freaked. Wild. Asking
for crazy shit, like a full-time bodyguard.
I told him, 'Do you really think we can spare
a soldier??'
He was emotional. 'Why not shoot me now? It will
be quicker.'
What could we do? What would you do?
The only thing I could think of was to give him
a cot in the base. Offer him his job back.
So he moved in.

FOSTER   Nassir was different, then. Broody, withdrawn.
Talking to no one.
He cracked in the middle of an interrogation.
A throwaway remark: the trigger.
We had a prisoner running his mouth; boasting how
HE was going to Paradise... unlike Nassir who he
said had chosen riches and Paradise in this life.
And that made Nassir go crazy. He put his fist
through the desk.
He says – 'Paradise? You call this Paradise? I'm
as much a prisoner as you. I live in the same cells.
I eat the same shitty food. You want to go home –
well, guess what...?'
I take him out of the booth.
Say, 'What the hell are you doing? You can't bring
your problems into work.'
'Work IS my problem.'
I say: 'Guess what. My tour's been extended by
six months. I miss my family, I want to go home
too, but I'm not bitching about it. We're in the
same boat.'
'The same boat? The same?? When this is all over,
you can walk away. You can go home. My home
doesn't exist any more.'

Lighting change, to indicate a shift in mood.

KASPER   Black Wednesday. Downtown.
           The 72nd are on patrol. The soldiers walk the
           dusty streets, bored.
           A local woman approaches. Dressed in local hijab.
           Handsome more than pretty.
           She speaks a little English.
           'Please sir, please sir.'
           One of the grunts, a popular kid called Frazer, stops.
           She has her hand out, 'Please sir.'
           She explains that her husband was killed in the
           war with Iran. His family kicked her out when he
           died. She needs money.
           Frazer's about to move on.
           She puts her hand between his legs. Grips him.
           Looks deep into his eyes. 'Please sir.'
           Frazer looks to his friends, 'What to do?'
           His friends laugh. Tell him to be quick. They'll
           cover.
           She leads him to a quiet, cool corner. Leans
           against a wall. He unzips.
           She raises her hijab above her head. Smiling.
           BOOM.
           The last thing he sees are the tubes of explosive.

FOSTER   Black Wednesday, they arrest everyone.
           Prisoners arriving on cattle trucks.
           Pushed and prodded at gunpoint by Frazer's angry
           colleagues.

           I see them arrive. Watching from the door of the
           hard site.
           Watching Vallay laughing and joking with the
           grunts.
           He leads the prisoners towards Tier 1A. And he's
           taking the guys from the 72nd with him.
           I steam after him.
           'Hey, whoa!! Vallay?? Have you lost your mind?
           You can't take them in there??'
           'They ain't doing nothing wrong.'
           'You can't allow soldiers from an attacked
           division to have access to prisoners.'
           Vallay rolls his eyes. As if *I'm* the bad guy.

'Sorry, guys.'
The soldiers disperse.
One of them shouts: 'Take good care of them
prisoners, you hear, Vallay? You know what I mean.
Really look after them… You're a photographer,
ain't you? We want pictures.'
Vallay knows what they mean. And he'll take
good care of them.
Oh yes he will.

ZOYA   I know what happened the night of Black
          Wednesday.
          The last time I saw Nassir, he told me.

          Seems he was in the prison yard, when he heard
          music. His *own* music.
          He'd left the tape in the player, and somebody was
          playing it. Loud.
          And so he followed the sound to Tier 1A.
          And saw…
          And saw a prisoner on the floor in a pool of his
          own blood.

          And saw Vallay and his buddies panting and
          laughing and dripping blood – none of it their own
          – from knuckles knees elbows and shoes.

          Vallay even asked him to take a picture.

          Nassir admitted he went crazy.
          Quite apart from everything else – they were using
          his music – in which he'd poured all his love and
          passion – to torture a guy.
          Said he was going to report them.

          And so they cuffed him. Bagged him. Threw him
          into a cell.

          He didn't witness what they did to the prisoner…
          But he heard it all. Lying in the darkness.
          I can't imagine… What sounds would you hear
          when a man is being beaten to death?

FOSTER   The morning after.
          Tier 1A was quiet. Everyone spoke in hushed tones.

All sharing a terrible secret.
They uncuffed Nassir. Offered him treats, Oreos
and Twinkies.
He stood straight up – came to find me.
Took me a while to register what he was saying.
That a prisoner had been killed in Tier 1A.

KASPER   Soon as I heard, I tore in to Tier 1A.
Prisoners naked. With shaved-off eyebrows.
Cuffed to their cots in agonising positions.
'WHERE ARE YOU???' I yelled. Didn't even
know who I was yelling for.
Burst into a booth. And find an OGA man.
'What are you doing to my prisoners?'
Straight back, he snarled, 'Don't you undermine me
in front of MY prisoners. *In here* – I am God. I am
the Almighty. The Department of Interior, Rumsfeld
himself, wants us to "work the dark side".'
So I say, 'And THIS is how you do it?'
And he says, 'You're passing judgement!?! You!!
The Senior Officer who fucks the Juniors. How do
you think that's going to play with the High
Command? Can't control the prisoners. Can't
control his guards. Can't even control his zipper.
…You've worked hard to get where you are,
Captain. This is a man's world. Think on that.'

FOSTER   I came to see him. He was cold.
I asked him what he was going to do about
Vallay.
He started defending him.
'Who got to you?' I said.
'No one,' he said, 'no one.'
He told me the OGA were doing a good job,
breaking down the Arab's sense of self with the
nudity, the panties…
And he rubbed his nose.
I said 'Come ON. Treating the prisoners like that
HARDENS their resolve. You know that.'
He turns on me. 'Get back to work, Sergeant
Foster. Your problem is you're too emotional, too
empathetic. You need to toughen up.'

They were all the clichés that men use when they object to women in the war zone.

So here we were. Trying to teach the Iraqis liberation. When we didn't even have it in our own ranks.

That was a bad day.

KASPER   I loved her. I now know I loved her. And I gave her up.

FOSTER   So I had to break the news to Nassir. That there would be no action against Vallay.
Now he had people who wanted to kill him outside the prison, and now he had Vallay on the inside.

I expected anger, I expected bitterness. But Nassir just retreated to his cell in silence.
He just kind of gave up. He even stopped playing his guitar.

We tried to give him his space, until he got his head straight, but that day never seemed to come.

I wanted him to come back to work. I did.
But eventually, he just became another Iraqi in a prison cell.
And even I stopped asking for him.

ZOYA   My father comes home one day with a black eye.
His clothes ripped.
He won't say what happened.
But I am forbidden to queue for petrol any more. That job must go to the men.
…Then he volunteers to do all my chores. To do the shopping. He doesn't want me leaving the house.
I sneak out one day determined to go buy some CDs…
There are men outside the house in mirror shades. Speaking into cellphones. I walk.
They follow.

I only get to the end of my street, and I'm running back home.
We're not safe any more.

I know one of the nurses at the base.
She is scared to be seen talking to me.
I plead with her, I beg her, bribe her to smuggle
a message to Nassir.
I tell him I love him.
I tell him we're scared.
I tell him we're not safe.
I plead for his help.

FOSTER   One day, Nassir received a letter from his fiancée...
And suddenly he volunteered to translate again.
I thought I would be excited.
But I didn't recognise him.
He was surly, arrogant. Wouldn't meet your gaze.
I really hoped he would come round.

KASPER   I thought we had the old Nassir back.
But I now know different.

When we interrogated high-ranking insurgents, he
was pretending to translate our questions.
But in reality he was asking questions of his own.

FOSTER   We interrogated this important local Bad Guy.
They called him The Falcon.
Nassir was passionate, animated.
A lot was said.
But when we asked for a translation, Nassir said
there wasn't any actionable intelligence.

ZOYA   It seems that when Nassir met The Falcon, he just
told him – directly – that he didn't want to work
for the Americans any more.
That he'd made a mistake.
All he cared about was...
Was protecting me.
And he would swear his allegiance if...
If The Falcon would protect me.

And so they made a deal.
Nassir was to take me to Faisal.
To Faisal!
...Faisal could, would, keep me safe.

And all Nassir had to do in return, was deliver
a package into the base. To The Falcon.

And when the Americans asked what The Falcon
was saying –
– Nassir replied, 'He only said, "You people can
go fuck yourselves".'

FOSTER   After The Falcon interview, Nassir said he had to
leave the base. To go see his fiancée.

KASPER   Didn't give it a second thought.

ZOYA   He arrived. I hadn't seen him for days, weeks.
He was different. His beard, his eyes – wild.
I tried to kiss him.
He said, 'We're going for a drive.'
There were three men in a car outside.
Mirror shades.
'You'll be okay,' he said.

They blindfolded us.
We drove.
For what seemed like an age.
The only sounds, the engine.
And on the car stereo.
Unknown to No One.
'Get up, get up, Let me hear you say, To the Father
of the People: Happy Birthday.'

We arrived at a compound.

The blindfolds were lifted.
The first thing I saw was the scar.
Faisal.
'He will look after you now.'
Faisal??
Faisal. To be my protector. The devil himself.
Faisal. My master.

Nassir swaps me for The Package.
The Package is a guitar case.
It's heavy.

'No one will question why a musician is carrying
a guitar case,' sneers Faisal.
The case is full of guns.

And then Nassir had to go.
'I love you,' he said.
I said nothing.

Now I must live with Faisal's mother in the
women's quarters. 'Safe.' 'Protected.'

We fought for freedom. And it led me here. To this
house. Where I am 'free'. 'Free' to cook and clean
for the men. 'Free' to be beaten if I leave the
house without male supervision...

I have kept a box of CDs – my secret collection –
which will get me whipped if it is found. For
music 'distracts the mind from Allah...'

This is my destiny. This is the destiny of all
women in Iraq. To live in someone else's house
under someone else's rules.

FOSTER   The guys on the gates were always paranoid.
Checked everyone. Maybe it's a measure of their
affection for Nassir that they trusted him. Perhaps
uniquely. Nassir, the singer. The funny guy. The
guy who sang songs in the Mortar Café. Who used
music to bring us together... Perhaps that's why
no one checked the guitar case.

It was December 16, 2003.

I'm assessing a new intake of prisoners – just
another day – when one of them spits in my face.
A bloody mouthful.
I want to just wipe it off, get on, cos there's too
much to do.
But one of the medics steps in. 'Not so fast,' they
say. 'You need to get checked out. Prisoner might
have TB.'
That's how I came to be in the sickbay THAT night.

KASPER   THAT night some of the guys from the 72nd were
           dropping off supplies.
           Some stopped in the Mortar Café.
           One of them sees Vallay, worrying a burger.
           'Hey, Vallay. Did you get those photos?'
           He did.
           Vallay produces the camera.
           All the guys from the 72nd crowd around.
           Laugh. And whistle.
           Pat his back.
           Vallay is pumped. He has an idea. Says: 'Foster's
           in quarantine for the next twenty-four hours…
           Wanna come up Tier 1A? See me in action?'

           In Tier 1A.
           Four naked prisoners. Specially selected, because
           of their part on Black Wednesday. Nervous.
           Clutching their cocks for comfort. Ringed by the
           team from the 72nd and Vallay.
           'Show us what you do, Vallay.'
           So.
           Keen to impress, Vallay knees the prisoner in the
           lateral side of the thigh. Hard. The prisoner falls to
           the ground. But they're not impressed.
           'Let me have a go,' asks a grunt called Blondie.
           'Nah, you ain't allowed to touch the prisoners,'
           says Vallay.
           Too late.
           Blondie stamps on the prisoner's knee.
           There's a crack, and the leg bends the wrong way.
           Over the screams, Vallay says, 'You can't do that,
           I'm gonna get into trouble.'
           But Blondie isn't listening.
           He stamps on the prisoner's face. It bounces.
           'Get the dogs in here. Make 'em bite the guy's
           dick off.'
           'Put dogfood on his balls. Ha ha ha.'
           'No no, guys, guys. Please stop. STOP.'

FOSTER   Am in quarantine, when this Iraqi kid from the
           café staff bursts in.
           'Get out of here. I may be infectious.'

'Miss, miss. It's Vallay. I hear him. He takes the
soldiers into Tier 1A.'
I didn't wait to be discharged.

KASPER   In the shadows in the cells in Tier 1A, the prisoners
watching, clutching steel, waiting for the moment.
Suddenly, the click-clack of claws.
A dog-handler has been found.
The naked prisoners shriek.
The grunts from the 72nd cheer. It's party time.
The noise, the noise is good. In the shadows the
prisoners use the noise to lock. And load.

FOSTER   And I tear into Tier 1A. And everything happens
in slow-motion.
And I see Vallay.
And the 72nd.
And snarls and hate.
And piss blood teeth.
And the steel.
And I'm screaming.
Then the gunshots.
Bang. The dog drops.
Bang. Blondie drops.
Prisoners screaming soldiers diving.
Bang bang. I drop.
And as my eyesight blurs into black, I whisper my
last words. No great oratory, no great speeches.
Just: 'What the fuck...?'

KASPER   A traitor in our midst: a gun-smuggler.
Two grunts dead. And Foster.
Who? Who was it? That brought guns in?
Find him.
Round up the Iraqi staff. Inspect their belongings.

Find him.
We find razor blades. Food. Drugs.
Messages to the outside.
But we don't find him.
Who's the traitor? Who?

My first thought was to warn Nassir, because he'd
be top of the Bad Guy's hit-list.
He was in his cell. C27. He'd shaved. Looked like
the old Nassir. Sitting on his bunk.
And I tell him, you need to wear your balaclava.
We got a traitor in the camp.
And he looks and says it's okay.
And I say you need to wear your fricking
balaclava.
And he says I don't want to wear it. Because it's
hot, it's itchy. And as he says this he rubs his nose.
Then covers his mouth… Sits on his hands.
…And I know. I KNOW.

And he knows I know. And I kick his guitar case,
and out come the bullets.
And he's running for the door. But one of the
grunts body-slams him.
And he's down,
And Vallay has his gun out. And he's pushing at
Nassir's temple.
'Shoot him', they say. 'Shoot him.'

And he can't. He can't.
And Vallay's crying. No longer the soldier. Now
the nineteen-year-old boy.

Let me. Let me.
I was going to break him.
And pulp him, and make him bleed. For Foster.
And so I hit him and I hit till my knuckles bled.
And I wielded the bat.
And I took the cloth and I covered his face, and
I poured the water.
And he was gasping and heaving like he was
drowning.
And then, and then, I commanded them to prepare
the room with the trapdoor.
And they put up the rope. Tightened the noose.
And made it good.
And he will suffer.
And I go fetch him, from his cell.

And I see his fear. And look in his eyes. And I hiss,
'Traitor. Traitor.'

But suddenly he laughs, and laughs.
And says: 'Me? The traitor? What values have
I betrayed?'
'You betrayed us.'
'No. You betrayed yourself. You people aren't the
Americans. I'm the American.'
And I think he's crazy, and I think the
waterboarding may have screwed his brain. And
I say, 'Where's your fucking passport then?'
And he says, 'To the world, America isn't a place or
a flag – it's a state of mind. America is justice, and
freedom, and liberty. The world needs America…
AMERICA needs America. You are the lie.'

And I stopped him talking, by pushing my gun
through his teeth.
And the room I shot him in was C27.
And when I pulled the trigger, his body fell with
a thud. An empty thud which never left us.
And I'm left with the absence. The soul-sucking
dark shadow. That will always be by my side.

ZOYA   We are combatants in the perpetual war
Which began here six thousand years before.
The seeds of our struggle were sown back then
The struggle that's embedded in the hearts of men.

For when we made the Cradle of Civilisation
We also grew anarchy, along with the nation.
And what sprouted out of our Fertile Crescent
Wasn't always good, wasn't always pleasant.
For our richest crop is political crisis
And our latest harvest is that of Isis.
But they aren't our real foe – nor Al-Qaeda, nor
Saddam,
The real foe is deep in the heart of man,
For the history of Iraq shows a chilling reality
That man's greatest enemy is our own brutality.

ECHOES

Echoes was first performed at the Gilded Balloon, Edinburgh, on 5 August 2015, with the following cast:

TILLIE	Felicity Houlbrooke
SAMIRA	Filipa Bragança
Directors	Henry Naylor
	Emma Butler

It was co-produced by Henry Naylor and the Gilded Balloon's Karen Koren.

The cast stayed the same for the subsequent world tour, until 13 September 2016, when Rachel Smyth replaced Felicity in the role of Tillie, for the shows at the Brisbane Festival and the Melbourne Fringe.

In April 2017, at the 59E59 Theater in New York, Serena Manteghi joined Rachel Smyth, and took the role of Samira.

To AGN,
For teaching me the love of history.

Characters

TILLIE, *a Victorian pioneer, seventeen*
SAMIRA, *a modern Muslim, seventeen*

The story of Echoes *is told by two different storytellers.*

They each deliver their monologues directly to the audience, through the 'fourth wall'.

Fade up on a young, Victorian pioneer woman, TILLIE. *She's strong, smart – seventeen years old.*

TILLIE   Three months at sea. The lump sugar is gone.
The eggs are rotten, and thrown overboard. India cannot come too soon.
At dinner a handsome Lieutenant approaches.
Winks conspiratorially. And presents me with a fig.
'Slipped the storemaster a few coins.'
I smile gratitude.
Then bite the flesh. There's a smell of rot, and the fizz of ferment.
A maggot inside. Wrestling with its own being.
'Oh. Oh, I'm so sorry,' blushes the appalled Lieutenant.
He would crush it. But I stay his hand.
'It is one of God's creatures!… Insects. Hobby of mine – and this one performs the most spectacular transformation in nature. More wondrous than the caterpillar… Blind, now, hopeless. But soon to grow wings, legs. Thousands of eyes.'
The Lieutenant snatches the fig, maggot and all, and crushes it in a puffed fist. Red juice running through his fingers.
'Flies are not suitable discourse for a lady.'

Fade up on a young, beautiful Muslim, SAMIRA. *She's strong, smart – seventeen years old.*

SAMIRA   I know what you're thinking:
'Why would a Grade-A student suddenly upsticks to become a housewife in a Syrian basement?'
Ha. You kuffar don't understand Faith, do you?

This is my choice: Paradise… or Ipswich.
The first: the shadow of God's kingdom on earth.
The second: a land of chip papers and dogshit.
You choose.

Wasn't always religious. Used to be shy, quiet.
A good student.
Until the day I sold Beegum a mousemat in
WHSmith's…

My Saturday job is manning the till, stacking the
shelves, in the News and Magazines section.
…Embarrassing to have to serve my devout
schoolfriend.
'Man, how can you sell this shit?' She waves her
hand over the newsracks.
'What's wrong with it?'
'Kuffar press is full of lies. Only times Muslims
get mentioned is when they're beheading people.
Never anything about the Syrian refugees, or
drone strikes killing babies.'
She may have a point;
the front pages are often about Kim Kardashian's
bottom.
'So how come *you* know about refugees, and
baby-seeking missiles?'
'Internet.'
'The internet!?! There's people on the internet says
that dress is blue/black rather than white/gold.'
'It is.'
'How can you say that?? It's white/gold.'
'Blue/black.'
…'White/Gold.'

Lunchtime, I look up 'Syrian refugees' on my
smartphone. There are three-point-eight million
of them.

I pretend to tidy the shelves. Flick through
a tabloid. Mostly the Election and Nigel Farage.
…The refugees only appear on page eleven. After
an advert asking whether I'm Beach Body Ready.

In another, there are no refugees.
Instead, there's a whole page of Katie Hopkins.
Flapping her mouth like a bag lady.
As the customers come and lay their papers on the
counter, I want to grab them and shout: 'Are we
not human to you?'
But what I actually say is: '…do you want the
vouchers?'

TILLIE   I must confess.
I was a maggot, once, writhing on a dungheap
called Ipswich.
Blind, wingless, directionless.
Thrashing around, trying to find a man. For my
Christian desire is to produce children for the
Empire.
But there are no men in Ipswich. Only a succession
of squinting dullards…

My latest suitor is Francis, the pasty son of
a leather manufacturer.
A ninny, who has taken exception to the railways.
'Heed my words, these "railways" are but a fad.
Some of these vehicles travel in excess of
twenty-five miles per hour.'
'Why is that so objectionable, sir?' I say.
He baulks. 'What lady is going to want to travel
at such ferocious speeds? Think of the damage to
their hairstyles.'
'Ah, nullum bonum valebat perdere lapsas.'
'Er, quite,' he says.
I smirk. 'It means: "Never let an adventure get in
the way of a good hairstyle".'

My father's jaw tense, as he bids Francis farewell.
'A capital woman,' says Francis, 'Capital. If only
she hadn't floored me with her Greek.'
My father shuts the door, his rage, palpable.
'You are too spirited. How many men of means do
you think there are in Ipswich?'
I look out on to the square. See the governesses
wrapped in their threadbare gloves and carpet bags.

Spinsters at twenty-five.
My destiny.

SAMIRA   Ask me who groomed me for jihad, I'd reply
Nigel Farage. I say this partly hoping that they'll
arrest him and put him in a cell with a sex-starved
simpleton called Bubba. But partly because he
pushed me to the Caliphate...

Morning of the General Election – we had a class
debate. Normally, I didn't really take part. But
then a boy called Piers said he'd vote for Farage.
'Farage????'
'We're about to enter the job market; we need to
limit immigration.'
'Farage said Muslims are a "fifth column"?'
'...Well, you can't dispute this, but the odd
Muslim has been known to blow shit up.'
'Well, the odd Christian has been known to fiddle
with children and sing "Two Little Boys" – but
that doesn't make them ALL Rolf Harris.'

That night. Watching the results on TV, depressed.
Ping. An email, from Beegum.
'Where do you belong? Here? Or in the Caliphate,
where we care for the Poor, and the Suffering?'
I don't reply.
By the morning, four million people have voted
for Farage. And the new government cuts benefits
for the Poor and the Suffering.

TILLIE   I'm in despond – when my brother Dashy returns
from India. After five years abroad, he's a man,
thick-set, handsome.
'Tillie?! My, you've become quite the young
lady... Father married you off yet?'
'There are no men in Ipswich, you know that.
The best are in India.'
'So join the Fishing Fleet,' he laughs.
'What's that?'
'There are four men to every woman in India.
It's a problem. The Company gives free passage

to women willing to marry the staff. They'd love
a bright young thing like you.'
'...really??'

SAMIRA   Saturday, WHSmith's. All about the Election.
The only story about Muslims? Deep in a tabloid.
In the holiday isle of Kos, there's been an influx of
refugees. Boat people. Mothers and children.
Without food, shelter.
The tabloid's angle? 'Britons' holidays are being
ruined by these vermin.'
A customer places a copy on the counter, says
cheerily, 'Just this please.'
I'm revolted. Appalled. 'Kuffar,' I hiss.

Two minutes later. 'Samira. Can I have a word?'
The Manager. Grave face.
'Did you just call one of the customers a "fucker"?'
I laugh.
I'm unemployed.

Ashamed. Daren't face my father.
I go to Beegum's house. We shut ourselves in her
bedroom, and spend the afternoon sharpening each
other's indignation. Looking up the Truth on the
internet.
Then Beegum shows me a tweet by one of the
sisters in Syria. Doing target practice with AKs.
'Housework in the Caliphate,' says the tweet.
'The Sisters Learn How To Take Out Some Trash.'
'Cool, huh,' says Beegum, carefully.
'Yeah,' I say, uncertain.
She pauses.
Then confesses: 'I'm going out there.'
Darkness in her eyes.
'Don't tell anyone... I'm getting married.'

She calls her fiancé on Skype. Lets me watch,
unseen, off-camera.
I'm shocked. He's *a man*.
'I have a friend who wants to come with me.
Can you find her a husband?'

He laughs. 'Give me a day or two.'
Signs off.
'If your husband ends up being better-looking than
mine, I'll kill you,' she says.
Ha ha. Best friends forever.

TILLIE   Evenings on the Lowther Castle. The Captain
invites the unmarried to dine together.
Tonight, the sheepish Lieutenant takes his seat
next to me.
'Sorry, ah, about yesterday. Just felt – wasn't
fitting – to discuss the life cycle of the fly.'
'Tell me, what *is* fitting?'
'Reading and books.'
'Very well.'
'So-oo, what have you been reading?' he ventures.
'A book about the life cycle of the fly.'
He smiles.
I continue, 'I am surprised you seek employ in
India, sir. You will find it hard to avoid the fly
there, in all its cycles. *"Tantum musca operatur ut
indefesse ut Anglus."*[1]
'*"Omnis Anglus et musca scit officium."*[2] Indeed,
I serve wherever my country sends me. For it is
God's work, to spread our peace, wealth and
civilisation through Commerce.'
His words please me.
'And what sends you to India?'
'MY Christian duty. I seek a husband.'
'Then I recommend you drop your discourse on
flies. Sweet-talk is never populated with maggots,'
he smiles.
'Maybe it should be, sir. "If music be the food of
larvae play on".'

SAMIRA   I'm supposed to meet my husband in Beegum's
bedroom. By Skype.

And now find myself waiting anxiously on her bed.
Wearing her full veil and shield. Waiting, waiting.
'Might not call tonight,' says Beegum.
'Connection's not always great.'

---

1 Only a fly works as tirelessly as the Englishman.
2 Every Englishman and fly knows his duty.

Suddenly a synthesised beat. A fizz of grain and
static. And Akeem appears.
He's about thirty. British, swept-back hair.
Gorgeous.
'Hello, sister,' he coughs, shyly.
'Hello. What time is it with you?'
'About twenty to eleven.'
'…So where are you?'
'At work. This is my office.'
He holds up his device, showing a battle-ravaged
street, pockmarked with shrapnel.
'Looks just like my workplace.'
'Oh?'
'WHSmith's in Ipswich.'
He laughs.
'Is it frightening?'
'No, sister, it is Paradise. Every day my heart is
filled with joy. We're fulfilling God's purpose.'
I smile, unseen under the veil.
'You wear your hijab every day?'
'Yes. When I leave the house, I put on the djellaba
and the veil.'
'You have a beautiful soul, sister. When you marry
me, I will make you a queen.'
Beegum breaks the connection, just before her
mum walks in.

TILLIE   That evening, the Lieutenant proposes to me.
'I will say no. I do not love him.'
Lady Connie frowns. 'Marriage is not about love.
It is an arrangement. This man has status and
prospects: you would be foolish to decline.'

SAMIRA   Mum contemplates me suspiciously. She *knows*.
'I want you to stop being friends with Beegum.'
'Why?'
'Your studies have suffered since you became
friends. If you want a decent job – '
'Women don't have to work.'
'What does that mean?'
'Nothing.'

'Is SHE filling your head with this nonsense?'
I retreat upstairs.

On Tuesday we go to Raqqa.

TILLIE   The Lieutenant and I are posted to Kabul.
The Afghan mission is important, we are told.
Our occupation 'protects the Indian trade routes
against Russian expansionism'. Or something.
…It is not my concern, politics is the domain
of men.
Besides, I have my own duties to perform.

I had heard many rumours about men's bodies.
That they were dreadful things. But on my wedding
night, I am more frightened by my own…
For I seem to have morphed into an another
animal altogether – one with liquid skin, and
unfamiliar scents.
And as I mewl and paddle, he clutches my face,
and says, 'God bless you, Tillie, for your duty and
your sacrifice. God bless.'

Over the next three months, he makes sure I do
my duty and sacrifice as frequently as possible.
In fact sometimes he is so keen for me to do my
duty and sacrifice that I worry his love of country
may be too great.

SAMIRA   Well, we did make it. Driving into Raqqa, a minibus
of six brides.
Streets are quiet. Rubbish piled high.
I'm wearing the niqab, the shield. Vision reduced
to a slit.
Men – the only colour. In Western clothes. Casual.
Short sleeves, bare arms. Beards not compulsory.
One even in a fucking Man United shirt.

We're to stay in a woman's hostel, till our fiancés
return from fighting.

Huge. Used to be a Christian's house. Now
property of Islamic State.
The others squeal, fight over bedrooms.

I try to phone home.
No reception. The hostel-keeper shrugs. 'The
mujahid blew up the phone towers.'
My stomach sinks. 'I need to tell my mum where
I am.'
She pats my shoulder. '*We* are your family, now.
We are your sisters.'

We can't leave the house without a male escort.
All we can do is housework, lots of housework...
After a week indoors, Beegum snaps.
'This is mental. To get here – you gotta be bold, an
adventurer, full of initiative. But they don't want
that. All they want is for you to be a toilet-cleaner.'
'We're to be wives and mothers. Read your Koran.'
'I came to kill kuffar.'
She scours the toilet furiously.
'Am going to join the women's police.'

TILLIE   Our first night in Afghanistan, I have my monthly
            curse.
            'Confound you, Tillie,' fumes the Lieutenant.
            'Sir...?'
            'The Empire needs children. We are on the verge
            of greatness, and you must produce...'
            I am shocked to hear such sharp words.
            'I do not know why my body is not performing its
            womanly function, sir.'
            'Try harder,' he snaps.

            He is despatched to Kandahar to quell
            a disturbance. I am alone in an officer's quarters.
            Childless.
            Indolent. Writing letters, reading.
            Bored bored bored.
            This is Ipswich in Asia.

SAMIRA   A fly bouncing on the ceiling, desperately trying
            to escape.
            He's back from the front. We are to meet, to go
            through the pre-marriage rituals: I must show him
            my face.

Buzz bounce buzz bounce, a noise like a migraine.
He enters, wearing a tie. Rebellious hairs bursting
through the warp and the weft of his ill-fitting
shirt; handsome, grinning too hard, chitter-
chattering with the chaperones.
And now the moment. My veil lifted. I coyly raise
my eyes.
He circles like a man inspecting a second-hand car.
A faint smile on his lips.
'I swear to Allah that I have not seen greater
beauty on this earth.'
I blush.
He coughs. Sniffs.
'I'm only on leave for a week. Can we get married
today?'
The fly lands on my face. I brush it away.

TILLIE   The Lieutenant returns.
We will go to the bazaars, to see the successes of
commerce.
We see patchy shops selling spices and silks.
Fruit shops.
With occasional sacks of apricots.
My fingers are enjoying their soft fur, when I see
an old beggarman.
In English, he hisses, 'What is your purpose here?'
I am taken off-guard. 'To be with my husband, sir.'
I look around for the Lieutenant. He is four stalls
distant, inspecting watermelons.
'"You" – the British. What is your purpose here?'
'To deliver charitable works through trade.' I need
to get away from this conversation.
But the old man grips my arm. 'Your "charitable
works" are not wanted here.'
A sudden crack from behind. Shoppers scatter.
Clearing a space for my horsewhip-wielding
husband.
'Unhand the lady, scoundrel!' he shudders.
'You? A fornicator? Ask ME to respect a woman?'
The Lieutenant flays the beggar across the face.
A red gash extending the mouth.

I scream.
The man raises his hands. Protests.
Whip-slash. Blood on fingers.
'Enough, enough,' I plead.
Whip-slash. Again. Again.
The beggar's face, a pulp.
'Stop, stop.'
But he can't. He is feral. Animal.
Whip-slash.
'Avert your eyes, Tillie. This is man's work.'
Smears and streaks on the ground. The grit-
covered flesh of ruined apricots.

SAMIRA I am to share the marital home with two other
females.
His first wife – and a young girl. Thirteen, maybe?
The former regards me with silent contempt.
I smile, friendly. 'Hello.'
She says nothing.
I imagine I am a threat. I am younger. Prettier.
Destined to share his bed that night.
I assume the young girl is their daughter.
She's not.
She's a Yazidi slave. She sleeps on the floor like
a pet.

On our wedding night, the acts we perform would
not have made me pregnant. But I'm keen to do
my duty.

I wait till he's sleeping.
Grope to the bathroom in darkness.
His seed, cooling on my back. I take some on my
fingers.
And push it into my body.
The dutiful wife.

TILLIE The Lieutenant rinses himself in a fountain.
'Impudent fellow. We do everything we can for
the betterment of these peoples.'
He shakes his hands, thinks himself clean. But has
a sanguine spray across collar and cheek.

'They never thank you.'

I am silent. Scared of his brutality.

'You going to say anything?'

'Your response was disproportionate, sir.'

He turns on me with fury, the animal still in his veins.

'What do YOU know? Why, if you had been alone with this savage, I can't imagine what he would have done to you.'

'The only savage here was you, sir.'

He punches me. Hard. A soldier's punch, practised in war.

SAMIRA   The next morning we go for a walk. Laughing newlyweds.

He takes me to the Al Ramah Square. We buy ice creams.

Walk across the seared grass.

Me – happy. Trilling like a bird.

Then, the smell. The sweet-sour scent of rotting meat.

Then, the fence.

Thin black rods, sharp finials.

On which are impaled human heads.

A bodiless boy.

Flesh dull lilac. The useless face slipping off the bone. Gravity melting the expression into a pantomime of despair.

A grotesque tourist attraction. My mouth fills with saliva.

I'm scared I might be sick inside my niqab. 'Can we go,' I plead.

But he won't.

'Eat your ice cream,' he says. 'It's melting.'

A power cut. The blades of the fan stilled. Air heavy. Rot feasting on the meat in the fridge.

'You ever beheaded someone?'

He shrugs, 'Of course.'

'Who was he…?'

'A Pagan.'

'A Devil-worshipper?'
'He worked for the Government.'
'That makes him a Pagan?'
He nods. 'There is only one ruler, and that is
Allah. We must govern according to his laws, or
be apostates.'
'Was he a brother?'
'He was Pagan.'
'Was he a Sunni?'
'It doesn't matter.'
'Matters to me. I'm relying on you to get us to
Jannah.'
He leaves the room. 'We're making the land pure.'
I shout after him, 'It is Satan's way. To get the
faithful to perform forbidden actions, in the name
of a "higher purpose".'
Slam. I'm talking to a closed door.

TILLIE   I must attend a cricket match: Artillery versus
Cavalry.
I attempt to disguise the bruise with powder.
But the gritty wind soon exposes my face.
The ladies whisper. But manners forbid comment.
I bury my chin in lacework.
A ripple of applause. A sweating Captain passes,
having scored fifty.
'Impressive knock,' I tell him.
He smiles.
'Not as impressive as the one on your cheek.
How'd you get that?'
The Lieutenant cuts in. 'A beggarman.'
'Your wife was attacked?'
I nod, eyes averted.
'We must find him, punish him.'
'I horsewhipped him myself,' says the Lieutenant.
'Well. He deserves worse.'
There's a ripple of applause, as a cavalryman hits
a boundary.

SAMIRA   One day, I'm sick. Vomiting up bile.
A common complaint.

The water purification plant has been broken for
months. Stomach pains are normal.
But the cramps worsen.
Wetness between my thighs. Hot. Sticky.
Blood.

…I wanted to do my duty – but my body didn't.

…My son was a rebel. A revolutionary. He defied
the state.
The Caliphate wanted him. But he resisted in death.

TILLIE   The bands strike. The thump of feet on the dance
floor. All around, they are dancing reels, jigging
jigs, making merry.
I am a reluctant celebrity. News of my assault has
spread – and gossip has rendered my assailant
increasingly savage.
One of the ladies drifts past saying – almost with
disappointment – 'Oh. I heard you lost an arm.'
I feel nausea. My body strains against the stiff
cocoon of corsetry.
To no one in particular, I say: 'I need to take
some air.'
Outside the tent, the night air is sharp, like a slap
of cold water.
I will borrow a burka from one of the camp
followers. Slip through the gates.
Find the beggar.

SAMIRA   I need my mum.
Reception. One bar. Enough.
'Hello?'
Her familiar voice. Through a sieve of static.
'Mum?'
'Samira…? Wait!'
A rustling of paper.
'Now. Listen.'
She reads me a script. The words of some 'expert'.
Tells me to forsake my hijrah. Says it is unIslamic
to disobey my mother. Quotes the Koran…
I can't listen.

They have destroyed us. Torn our umbilicus with savage force.
I hang up.

TILLIE   Outside the deserted apricot stall.
On the ground, the blackest of stains. A tar created by my husband's brutality.
The smear leads to an alley. Dark, impenetrable.
'Sir?' I shout into the blackness. 'Sir? Are you there? I have come to give you my apology.'
Did I hear a stirring?
I bluster. 'We are not all like my husband, sir.
Our intentions are pure. We have come to do God's work.'
Something thumps towards me.
Suddenly. In the moonlight: a gargoyle's face.
Speckled with dried blood, squinting through pulp and swelling.
The beggar.
'So. You are doing God's work, are you?'

I follow him to a deserted market square. The storekeepers gone.
Women and children, scrabbling in the dirt.
Sallow skin loose on yellow bones. Trying to find abandoned food.
An apricot, flattened by a dozen feet fought over by two young girls.
'Before the British, we were not beggars. But in the name of your Commerce, our farmers stopped growing food.'
'Why?'
'They grew poppies. So that you could sell opium to the Chinese.'
'But there is food in the stores?'
'Only for the rich. You British buy supplies at stupid prices. Everything cost more until this happens…'
The stench of rot and decay and death.

SAMIRA   No electricity. Shutters drawn.
Nothing to do but pray, and pray.

I hear explosions all day. The Mujahid are
blowing up the ancient temples downtown.

I go to the roof, watch as Inanna's Temple is
reduced to dust.
It survived five thousand years – now gone in an
afternoon.
A nation used to prostrate themselves before her
divinity. Now: nothing left.
Unease in my stomach.
In five thousand years' time – would they be
blowing up the mosques?
I'm panicked. Doubting is apostasy.

TILLIE   I fear a beating for my absence.
But when I return, the Lieutenant is not there.
He stumbles in at four o'clock. The fuzzy scent
of gin. Damp, and covered in mud.
Fear makes me sharp.
'Where have you been?' I snip.
He shakes his head.
'Did you fall in a ditch?'
No reply.

The dark is intense.
I think he's asleep.
I'm not. My thoughts slipping to the starving girls
I'd witnessed that night. Perhaps I could steal food
for them from the kitchens?
The Lieutenant's breath hasn't yet adopted the
rasp of sleep. I look across, see cold light
reflecting off an eye.
'You awake, Tillie?'
'Yes,' I say.
'In the morning, there may be people wondering
where I was, last night. Could you say we were
here?'

SAMIRA   My husband's idea of foreplay is to show me
YouTube videos of himself. I think he imagines
I'll be impressed.
'Watch this.'

He's tying a string of explosives round the necks
of ten 'Pagans'.
'Watch.'
BOOM!
'Boom! Look at the heads flying in the air.' He
laughs, seeking approval.
I feel sick.
'Where in the book does it tell you to do that?'
He looks puzzled.
' – these are kuffar – '
'The books says: "Whoever kills an innocent
human being, it is as if he kills all mankind" – '
' – Shut up, woman.'
Can't. Don't. Won't.
'I have always obeyed the men. It's what the book
commands.
But you are not men. You are ten-year-old boys
playing with a train set of explosives.'
His face murderous.
A blur.
Suddenly I'm on the floor.
Deaf. Ears ringing. Mouth filled with blood.
I try to push myself up. But he's on top of me.
His weight pins me… Hands everywhere.
Slapping, tearing.
Punches the back of my head.
Cool air on my exposed behind.
The jingle of the belt buckle.
I'm outside of myself.
Apart. Numb. A living cadaver.
Who observes, as evil forces inside.

TILLIE   I take tea in the morning with the wives. There are
cakes, scones, sandwiches.
I have a large purse, into which I will sweep
leftovers.
'Have you heard, Tillie? That we are to be
reassigned to China?
Seems the Chinese have been confiscating our
opium ships. They want us to teach them a lesson.'
I drop a finger sandwich into my bag.

'So what will happen to the Afghans?'
A shrug of the shoulders.
'The caravan moves on.'
'I'm sorry, but we have left people starving
outside the walls. Because we have played havoc
with the food prices. Shall we not stay and put
this good?'
Embarrassed silence.
Lady Grayston sniffs, holds forth.
'If these savages cannot perform simple
housekeeping, we cannot be held accountable.'
'So we are to neglect them... to deal opium in
the East?'
I slip another sandwich into my bag.
'Hungry, Tillie?' sneers Lady Grayston. She offers
me her tea plate. 'Perhaps you would like to add
my sandwiches to your purse?'
My subterfuge discovered, I stand, upend a whole
plate of cakes in my bag.
'No, madam. I am not hungry. I am going to take
these to the people beyond the wall, because I will
not neglect my Christian duty.'
'Your duty, Miss Tillie, includes decorum,' flares
Lady Grayston.
I show her my back, addressing the others, 'Did
your husbands ever have any Christian intent?
Or have they mocked our sacrifice?'

SAMIRA   The buzz of neon.
'I am torn, doctor. I need stitches.'
The doctor busy, efficient, crisp.
'Let's take a look. Keep the veil on, but lift your
abaya.'
She pulls on gloves.
I seize her wrist.
'Doctor. Please. I need contraceptives. I cannot get
pregnant to this man.'

TILLIE   My bag bursting with confections, a small gift for
the starving. I scuttle towards the gates.
The fight with Lady Grayston has left me
strangely exhilarated.

Which is perhaps why I didn't hear the protestors
till I was upon the gates.
'Ma'am, you must withdraw,' says a gatekeeper;
'Natives aren't happy.'
'Why?'
'Apparently we've "offended their honour"', he
rolls his eyes. 'Some of the lads had too much to
drink last night. "Had Their Way" with a couple of
local girls.'
My mouth is dry.
'Who did it?'
'No one's saying. Apparently one of the lads was
married. If these bastards find out who, they'll
stone him. Devils, they are.'
I can scarce breathe.
'Know where my husband is?'
'Went to celebrate the China posting with the
Deputy. If he's got sense he won't come back till
it's calmed down.'
But it doesn't calm down.

Cavalrymen are dispatched to drive back the crowd.
They fail. The press of fury: too intense.
A Captain attempts authority; but his voice is
deadened by the seething mass.
Missiles are thrown.
Horses jerk against bridles.
Hooves click-clack.
I push into the crowd in my burka-disguise.
Helpless. Carried by the swirls of the mob, like
a leaf in a storm. Bobbing this way, that.

I struggle free, like a creature born of a cocoon.
Damp.
Tired from exertion.
Fires and flames in the street.
He had his way. I will have mine.

SAMIRA   Seven stitches and a packet of Azurettes.
His first wife says nothing. But dresses my wounds.
'How do you endure him,' I whisper.
'What he did is halal. We must be obedient.'

'He raped me.'

'Sex is part of marriage,' she replies.

'Look what he did to me! – '

' – you are *lucky*,' she barks, firmly. 'But for your
injuries, he would have divorced you, and moved
on to the next woman. Women like you get passed
from fighter to fighter.'

'That is permitted??' I gasp.

'It's "sexual jihad". To get round the adultery
laws, the fighters marry a woman for a week, then
get a cleric to "divorce" them… He's done it
before.'

I laugh, coldly: 'The men, the men seem to be able
twist the rules when it suits them. And yet for us,
the law is rigid.'

A smile. But the eyes are dead.

'They hold the guns.'

TILLIE   I bang on the gates of the Deputy's compound.

'Open up!'

Surprised by an English voice, a servant unbolts
the gates.

I fly past. In the courtyard, a tinkling fountain,
carpets and bolsters at its base. The signs of
a picnic. Hooka pipes. Discarded clothes…

…His jacket.

'Where are you?!'

Burnes, the Deputy, emerges from an arcade.
Pained by sunlight, buttoning his shirt.

'What is the meaning of this?'

'Where is my husband?'

The Lieutenant emerges. Carrying his breeches.

'Tillie, is that you?'

A scurrying behind. Two whores, crouching over
their nakedness, rush to the house.

'How lovely to see you.' He licks cracked lips.
Attempts to speak with dignity, whilst fumbling
with trouser buttons.

'Eh. I know you're probably angry. Well you
mustn't be. Take this as a compliment. See, as
a man I have a natural impulse, which, out of

respect, I must perform sparingly with you. See?
You are a lady, a guardian of morality, and must
only fornicate for the duty of God and children,
and we must maintain your virtue, so that when
those children come, you may teach them God's
purpose. See?'
My silence incenses him. Turns him spiteful.
'That is, if you COULD produce a child... For
I fear you are barren.'
My mind searing, my words cool. 'Sir, I am proud
of my body. For its wisdom. Because delivering
a child for YOUR Empire would betray my duty
to womankind.'
He twitches.
'Tell me. What. Did. You do? To those girls last
night?'
He goes to the fountain. Adjusts his collar. Rounds
on me.
'It was your fault, you know. Where were you at
the dance? Looked everywhere. Couldn't find you.
So what am I supposed to do?... Partook of gin,
didn't I? With the Captain... Course, one thing led
to another. Went looking for that beggar, to teach
him "what for"... Couldn't find him... On our
way home – there were two girls. Probably
prostitutes. Captain said, let's see how THEIR
women like it... Took them to a water channel,
and – ... Boys will be boys, eh?'
...I am gone.

SAMIRA   One bar. Enough.
'Hello?'
'Mum.'
'Samira...?'
A rustle as she fumbles for a speech.
'No, stop – MUM!'
The rustling stops.
'I want YOU, Mum, not some social worker's
prepared speech. Scream at me, shout at me, tell
me I've been stupid... Just be YOU.'
'...Are you okay, Sammy?'

And suddenly the tears come.
'I want to come home, I hate it. I hate it. I love you, Mum.'
'You must get to Irbil. I'm going to give you an address… There are people who can get you out.'

TILLIE   I had believed the vision of Empire. The vision of men. Full of high ideals, and strictures of faith. So binding for women. Too loose for men.
No more. No more.
I have eyes which see everywhere. I have wings to fly. I am the Betrayer.

Standing at the edge of the mob, I shout, 'I know where he is – the Fornicator.'
My voice, small amongst the rage, but one man hears, understands.
'I know where he is,' I shout again.
He translates for his fellows. A buzz begins.
Which grows. And crystalises. And expands.

SAMIRA   Hot days waiting for a chance to escape. No power. The air-con: silent; air thick and still.

Then:
The night of the air raids.
Buzzing. Drones in the city. Explosions downtown.
Frightening and powerful.

I feel the energy in the air, like a dog before an earthquake.
This is the moment.

My husband has married a Tunisian 'bride' on a week-long contract. He's grunting and truffling in the marital bedroom.

I find his keys in his discarded trousers. Unlock his ammo store. Grenades, bullets and an AK.

I force the door of the marital bedroom.
His hairy arse shunting between milk thighs.
Body like a bear.
'Get OUT!'

I smirk, raise the AK.

Everything is still. His eyes wide. A snapshot of time.

I try to pull the trigger – it's stiff – doesn't move – try again – nothing.

He charges.

Come on come on –

' – out of the way.'

The first wife.

A grenade in hand. The pin jingles to the floor. She steps forwards. Embraces her husband. The grenade between them.

BOOM. A sudden belch of hell.

On the floor.

Can't see, can't hear.

A gritty fog of dust. Cracks in the plasterwork. A streak up the wall.

Ears ringing.

The Tunisian's mouth wide, must be screaming. Her chest open – her ribs. She raises her arm to the wound. Then crumples over the dismembered bodies.

…His head detached. Behind the mattress.

TILLIE   Then.

'Justice, justice, justice for the girls!'

I lead a swarm of anger. To Burnes' house.

We test the gates.

Surge into the neighbour's house. Climb on to the roof. Drop into Burnes' compound.

Justice justice justice for the –

Burnes stands in a window. Pleads for calm, offers bribes.

Gunfire. The shutters shatter. He retreats.

Justice justice justice for –

The gates are forced.

Confusion inside. Men this way and that.

Plunder and booty.

A man stealing a chair.

Justice, justice, justice – shots from the house.

Some officers, disguised. Attempt escape.

I point them out. 'Seize them.'
Blades slash. Hacking bone.
A sword is dropped. I take it.
Justice justice –
Flames in the house now.
Burnes is burning.
Heavy smoke. Coughing.
I enter. Determined to find the Lieutenant myself.
Inside.
The only occupants: smoke, and thieves.
Two servants with a heavy carpet.
A very heavy carpet.
Wait. Burnes' servants.
'What's in that carpet?'
They panic. Drop it. Run.
The carpet thuds and groans.
I slash. A yelp. Blood through the cut.
I unfurl.
The Lieutenant.
Dazed.
'Tillie? Is that you?'
'No longer,' I say.
And deliver the final blow.
Justice.

SAMIRA   'We're going,' I tell the Yazidi.
'We need a chaperone.'
'You have me.'

We bind my chest to flatten my breasts.
Find a razor, shave the dead man. Carefully glue
clippings to my chin.
Look in the mirror.
I am a man.
Not perfect, but passable.

We take a taxi.
Pass three checkpoints, on Akeem's ID.
No one looks closely. They see the word
'commander'. Wave us through.
My Yazidi wife's excitement is rising.
Checkpoint four should be the last.

You don't need to see a face to recognise
someone. Posture is unique. Movement. You can
recognise someone in an abaya.
…Beegum. Is working the checkpoint for the
women's police.
Oh no. Oh no.
My mind: scrambled.
Beegum will inspect the Yazidi.
I'm led to the male, Hisbah building.
Inside: the flag. A smell of sweat. Dirty plates,
pink with watermelon juice.
A checkpoint guard lazily takes the ID.
The glue feels itchy on my face. Desperate to
scratch.
'You are going to Irbil? What does a Briton want
in Irbil?'
'My wife's family.'
He hands the documents back.
I hold my breath.
He waves me away. We're going to make it.
For some reason Kool & The Gang's 'Celebration'
plays in the jukebox in my mind.
I'm almost skipping back to the cab.
'Celebrate good times, come on.'
Then, a cry from the women's booth. Beegum's
voice.
She has seen the Yazidi's tattoos.
'This girl is not Muslim.'
Oh no, not now.
'It's okay. She is Yazidi. She converted,' I shout.
Beegum flinches. She recognises me.
Silence.
The guard asks to see my papers again.
'I am taking my wife to Irbil,' I tell Beegum,
urgently. 'In a large taxi. I have room for a
second wife.'
Tension in her shoulders. She's listening.
I hiss, 'Best Friends Forever.'
The guard holds up the ID, compares my face.
Shoot him, I think. Shoot him.
'This isn't you,' he says.

'Shoot him, Beegum! SHOOT HIM!!'
She's frozen.
Then she whispers... 'Apostate'.

TILLIE   They worked his body to shreds of bone. His torso
left abandoned in the street.
Soon the smell of rot, the fizz of ferment.
His headless torso the playground of flies.

As with him, so with all the British.
In their arrogance they never imagined the
Afghans would attack. They built their stores
outside the cantonment. Undefended.
I show the swarm the way. Within minutes, the
garrison loses its food supply for the winter...

They will starve, the British. Be reduced to boiling
sheep skins and consuming grains from the
excrement of animals.
The mighty, eating like insects...
I will not survive the winter. Flies never do.

SAMIRA   I should be sitting my A levels now:
Instead, I'm sitting in a woman's jail. Awaiting my
final examination: in the courts.
Tomorrow, men will make the ultimate decision of
my life. The decision of its ending.
No. No more.
I have been the plaything of men for too long.
Now, *I* will decide my destiny. I will decide when
I die, not them. In Death, *I* will be victorious.

Beegum visits. Rigid with contempt.
'I have come to say goodbye. Safe to assume
I won't be seeing you in Jannah,' she sneers.
Heavy silence.
Then I smile, 'Remember when we first talked
about coming here? We talked about caring for
Muslims? Since I've been here, I have seen the
brothers stoned, beheaded, whipped, and pushed
off buildings... Have we protected them? Whose
side are we on?'

Beegum parries. 'We are acting on the Word.
The Word is perfect.'
I look down at my feet. Align them so they are
symmetrical.
Level my gaze.
'The Word is perfect. But the ears of men are not.
We hear the Divine voice, and try to replicate it.
But we can't. We're mortal. Speckled with agenda
and self-interest. The best we can do is produce an
echo. A distant, distortion of sound. Blurred,
imperfect. Repeated with flagging confidence.
Fading to nothing.'
Silence, darkness. Dense as iron.
I raise my hands together.
'Remember this – Satan is smart: he can't attack
Allah, so he attacks His people instead. Look
around you. Are you behaving according to
Allah's will or Satan's? Are you performing the
work of Allah the merciful?'
'You will burn in Hell,' she hisses.
'One of us will,' I say. 'Because at least one of us
is wrong.'
'...And that dress is blue/black!' she shouts.
'The dress,' I counter, 'must be more colourful
than that; the dress could be red/green.'

TILLIE We are the great artists. The creators.

SAMIRA Who from men's tiny seed fashion toes, arms,
legs. Minds.

TILLIE We created good, we created evil.

SAMIRA We created Men.

TILLIE And they would destroy us.
Gag us. Contain us. Limit our voices.

SAMIRA Reduce our vision to a slit.

TILLIE That is their everlasting war. With us.

SAMIRA ...She leaves me. Alone in the dark.
My abaya is fastened by a pin. I remove it.

Plunge the needle into my wrists, deep enough to
touch bone. And fighting the resistance of flesh,
drag it down.
My life flowing on to the floor.
I must move quickly. When they find me, they
must find a person.
Confront my humanity. My femininity.
They must see I had breasts, arms, hands and
expressions.
For this is my connection, the community of
humanity.
So with my last strength, I remove my abaya, the
T-shirt beneath. Shoes, underwear.
And before life slips away, I lean against the wall,
naked.
Beach. Body. Ready.

ANGEL

Angel was first performed at the Gilded Balloon, Edinburgh, on 3 August 2016, with the following cast:

REHANA, THE ANGEL	Filipa Bragança
Director	Michael Cabot

It was co-produced by Henry Naylor and the Gilded Balloon's Karen Koren and Katy Koren.

In the subsequent tour of Australia (beginning at Mittagong Playhouse on 7 February 2017) Rehana was played by Avital Lvova.

*Dedicated to the memory of Filipa Bragança,
the first Angel.*

A great friend and a wonderful colleague.

*Filipa was politically very committed, passionate
in her desire to make the world a better place.*

*And her stunning performance was important
in turning this show into a success.*

*The play was written with Fil in mind, and hopefully
it captures some of her wonderful spirit.*

May her friends always retain her sun in their hearts.

Character

REHANA, *Kurdish, nineteen*

The story of Angel *is entirely told by* REHANA, *who tells her autobiographical story directly to the audience, through the 'fourth wall'.*

Lights up on a young REHANA. *She's looking for something. Breathing heavily, panicked; she's been running.*

REHANA   Snarls and yelps amongst the trees.
                 A desperate fight for life.
                 The air hot and fetid in the orchard, like
                 a predator's breath.
                 'Bizou? Bizou?' I cry.
                 I am twelve. Running through the pistachios.
                 'Where are you, Bizou?'
                 I find the dog limping, bleeding.
                 Circled by a huge jackal. Foaming, bloodied
                 muzzle.
                 The monster twitches. Shakes its head at the sky;
                 sowing drools of madness into the soil.
                 Then turns fury on me.
                 Snarling, baring teeth. It charges, leaps.
                 I flinch expecting its bite.
                 A zip. Thud.
                 …suddenly, the jackal's head explodes in a spray
                 of blood and tissue.
                 What…??
                 Am stupid with shock. Gaping like an idiot.
                 The jackal, leaking red, into the thirsty soil.
                 'Angel, Angel! You okay?!'
                 My father.
                 Running up, sniper rifle in hand.
                 He hugs me ferociously.
                 'You bitten?'
                 'No.'
                 '…Bizou?'
                 Poor Bizou, limping, showing me the whites of
                 his eyes.

'...Yes.'

'Aye aye aye,' he says, sadly. 'There is nothing we can do for him.'

He holds the gun out, says gently. 'Shoot him.'

'What...?'

'Shoot Bizou. This is a lesson you must learn.'

The lights change. Suddenly REHANA *steps out of the scene, addresses the audience directly, and conversationally.*

She's strong, confident, smart – mature beyond her nineteen years: a Kurdish Amazon warrior.

If you haven't heard of Kobane, it's okay.

Not many people have.

It's a bland border town where nothing used to happen.

Like Berwick-upon-Tweed[1], in Syria.

And had Kobane been one kilometre further north, in Turkey, nothing would have happened.

For one year Kobane was the most important place on earth: the front line of the battle between Freedom and Tyranny.

The reason you barely know about it?

The journalists all fled, lest they were beheaded.

The sacrifice and heroism of our brave women: trees falling in an unreported forest.

So. Lest it's forgotten, here's our story.

I'm Rehana. The Angel. From the village of Tall Ghazal, twenty miles south of Kobane...

And suddenly the lights change. Sunny, optimistic. REHANA *is a year younger, infinitely more naive and girlish. Not hard-bitten.*

The next time I see the gun, I'm seventeen.

The sun is stealthy and low, about to burn off the sweet dew of an Arab spring.

When my father starts firing the gun on the porch.

Whooping like a madman.

---

1 We'd change the name of the 'bland' town, according to whichever country/region we were performing in. Turn it into a local reference to amuse the audience.

'What are you doing, you silly old fool?' yells
my mother.
'We are free, my dove. West Kurdistan has
declared independence!!'
He kisses the top of my head.
'You won't have to fight for liberation, my Angel,
like I did!'
He spent six months, fighting in the mountains;
and thirty years banging on about it.
'When Assad gets his strength up, he'll take us
back.'
He ignores me. 'In this country, women will be
truly the equal of men.'
'God forbid I become your equal. My IQ would
have to drop by a hundred points.'
'What do you mean – ?… No one will question
when you take over the farm.'
I look over the regimented trees, and shudder. 'I'm
going to be a lawyer, Dad.'
A grunt of irritation.
'Like William Shatner in *Boston Legal*?' offers
my mother.
'William Shatner?? Thought he was a spaceman?'
'…Ye-s.'
'With the friend with the pointy ears?'
'Yes.'
'Says Nanoo Nanoo Shazbat?'
I can't help laughing. He rarely watches
television, he's a farmer.
'It's "Beam Me Up Scotty".'
'"Beam Me Up Scotty?"Aye aye aye. My daughter
wants to be William Shatner? Aye aye aye.'
He still thinks my passion for the law is a childish
phase.

Mid-September.
The villagers helping with the annual harvest.
Children chirruping and laughing, seeking the
most productive trees.
I'm going to win, I have intimate knowledge of
our orchard.

I know where Benny's tree is: the grandfather of
them all. The one supposedly planted three hundred
years ago, by my ancestor Benny Ghazali.
But when I get there, there are strangers
occupying the branches.
Elder boys. Teenagers. Wispy beards and thin
moustaches. I only recognise the ringleader –
a religious hothead, called Wahid.
'You can't come in here,' says Wahid, with disdain.
'There is room in this tree for all of us,' I say
reasonably.
'You are a girl. You should be indoors. And your
hair should be covered.'
'Your ugly face should be covered, but I'm not
going on about it.'
I make to climb. But he plants a kick in my face.
Smirks all round.
'This is my family's tree.'
He shrugs. Not his problem.
Angry at the injustice, I run to my father, tears
now flowing.
He listens to my story. Is angry.
With me.
'This is your house, you tell them – '
'You don't know what it's like to be a girl, faced
with a pack of men – '
My father bellows irritation.
Picks up the machete he uses for harvest.
Marches purposefully to the base of the tree.
Broad shoulders pressing the seams of his shirt.
The youths silenced by his approach.
'Get down,' he says firmly.
One of the boys makes to jump, but Wahid
stops him.
'What do you want, old man?' he sneers.
'Get off my farm, get out of my tree.'
Wahid laughs. 'Make me.'
A twitch in my father's jaw.
'Look at me,' he commands, with authority.
He raises his palm.

Slaps into it the flat of the machete. Curls his
fingers round the blade. Grips it. Tight.
'Look. At. Me.'
Then slowly my father draws the knife out of his
fist-sheath.
Opens his palm, so all can see. A deep groove,
filling purple and overflowing.
An ugly flap of skin hanging down.
Through all this, my father has not blinked once,
nor shown pain, nor looked away.
'Get out of my tree,' he says calmly.
Wahid – pale.
Silenced.
Jumps down.

Next morning, as I'm getting changed, my father
shouts through the bathroom door, sunnily.
'School is cancelled, Angel.'
'What? Why?'
'There's been an outbreak of sickness,' he says.
I open the bathroom door, my father is waiting:
the rifle on his shoulder, a six-pack of Orangina in
his bandaged hand.
'Thought we could use the time constructively.'
'Drinking Orangina???'

He places the cans in a line, on top of a tree
stump, three hundred metres distant.
Then approaches, offering the rifle.
'Okay, shoot the cans,' he says.
'WHAT?? Impossible.'
His mouth makes a hard line. He raises the gun,
shoots. One of the cans drops.
Even in my teenage sulk, I'm impressed.
'Shoot the cans.' He proffers the gun.
'Girls shouldn't hold guns.'
'Nor should men,' he says gruffly.
He moulds my hands around the weapon.
'Most important thing: control your breathing.
The slightest movement affects your aim.'

I squeeze the trigger. Miss. And enjoy it.
'Happy?'
'Again.'
And again. And again.
'Can we stop now?'

But the 'sickness' at school lasts and lasts.
Each morning, down the fields, moulding my aim.
Each morning I miss. And miss.
His frustration rising. 'You're thinking too much,'
he says. 'Stop thinking.'
'Why are we doing this?'
'To prepare.'
'Against what? Against an army of fizzy drinks?'

Day four, I hit my first can.
We both whoop.
As a reward, he tries to teach me the liberation song.
'Comrades Unite, for we will be free, come shed
your blood for Kurdistan.'
This is a step too far. 'I'm not singing *that*.'
'Aye aye aye. Why not?'
'Hardly Beyoncé.'
'I'll sing one of yours, if you sing mine.'
'Okay, me first. "All the Single Ladies" – '
His lip curls miserably. Sings: 'All the Single
Ladies – '

After ten days, one in five shots are hitting.
After twelve: one in three. One shot even went
through the dot of the 'i' in Orangina. My father
almost smiled.
'Can I go back to school yet?'
He says nothing. Just moves the cans back an
extra hundred yards.
'This is your education.'
' – I'm not going to get into law school, unless – '
' – When you hit six out of six – '
'Has there even been sickness in school?'
'Shoot the can. Shoot it.'
'No.' I throw down the gun.
'Pick it up.'

'NO.'

'How can you run a farm if you can't defend it from predators?'

'I'm never going to run the farm.'

He tuts. 'Is this Shatner's fault?'

'It's nothing to do with William Shatner.' I turn on him unreserved fury.

'Farming's a fool's game. You toil and toil, and what do you get in return? Failed crops, parasites, and pets which catch rabies. Nature's a monster. Much better the reasoned judgements of men, than the arbitrary, amoral shitty Rules of Nature.'

'You think you can place humans above Nature? Humans are animals. And as an animal, you have only one decision to make... Are you prey or are you predator?'

He gets out more cans.

Day Thirteen, I run away. To school. I'm the opposite of a truant.

For most kids, teenage rebellion manifests itself in wild haircuts. Vicious music. I rebel by being a swot.

My father bristles at my obstinacy.

He recognises a streak which took him up to the mountains to fight.

And it enrages him.

He knows my will can't be broken.

Midsummer. Night-time. Heat still fierce.

Hot sweat sticky on my skin. A burning tar, too intense for sleep.

Across the fields, cicadas chirruping a warning. I need water, pad to the kitchen.

Find my father by the open back door. The radio on.

'What are you doing?'

My father wipes his eyes.

'Mosul has fallen.'

'Mosul? In Iraq?'

'The Iraqi Army ran away.'

'Stupid Iraqis.'

'Left their weapons behind. Daesh have taken
them all. Over four thousand machine guns,
Howitzers – '
The numbers mean nothing to me, I don't know
what a Howitzer is, Mosul is miles away.
'Poor people.'
My father stands angry.
Snatches one of my textbooks from the sofa, and
hurls it across the room.
Without saying anything, he takes a lantern into
the trees.

Begins trimming branches in the dark.
Jeered at by an army of insects.
'Why you pruning now?'
Clip clip clip.
He snarls bitterly into the tree's dark centre.
'See this tree? Wonder why it never has any fruits
on it? That's because it's a pollinator. A male tree.
Only the females bear fruit. There are fools who
think it's okay for the pollinators to have all the
sun, all the fertiliser, all the water. Whilst planting
all the fruit-bearing trees unwatered in the dark.'
He slaps his palm against the rigid bark.
'These people should never be allowed a farm.'

He works all the night. Burning the trimmings.
Standing close to the flame. Alone.

I'm having a lie-in. I earned it, just won a place at
law school. My reward, a few days without study.
'Rehana, get up.'
As I swim into consciousness.
Crackles. Bangs. Thumps. Across the fields.
A firework display at daytime?
'Rehana, get up.'
My mother, flustered at the door. Her scarf pulsing.
'We're going away. Get packing.'
She throws me one of the hessian sacks used for
harvest; farmers never have holidays; we've no
suitcases.
'…?? Where are we going?'

'Europe.'
'Europe??'
Now she's banging cupboards, making snap
decisions on clothes, ornaments and jewellery.
' – Daesh are coming.'
In the orchard, a startled rabbit scampers.

Horns blaring like an expletive, a farm truck
arrives, demanding urgent departure.
Driven by the neighbours: old man Hassan, the
women and children.
No free seats in the cabin. We are herded on to the
flatbed, where we will travel with some crates of
alarmed chickens. The tailgate is slammed behind.
'Where's Dad?'
'The men will follow later, Angel.'
The vehicle splutters to life.
I use my sack as a seat. The lumpy corner of
a textbook providing no comfort.
I'm as twitchy as the chickens.
Black smoke on the horizon behind.
Must run, must run.
'We'll be okay, Angel,' says mother. 'They'll look
after us in Europe.'

Daylight dying with a lilac beauty.
We've been waiting to cross the border for three
days, huddling in dusty fields.
The Turks won't let us over.
'We are full,' a guard said. 'If we let in one of you,
we have to let you all in.'
One hundred and thirty thousand of us, waiting for
them to change their minds.

I can find no rest on the hard-baked earth.
'He stayed to fight, didn't he?'
My mother shifts uncomfortably.
'Stupid, stupid, they'll kill him, behead him.'
She shrugs. 'You know your father: he is stubborn.'
'What's he *thinking* of?'
'He stayed to fight. For the trees.'
'For "some trees"?'

'Not "some" trees. The family's trees; your trees.
He feels the responsibility. Of being the custodian.
Wants to make sure they're safe to pass on.'
'…To me?'
She doesn't answer.
'He knows I don't want to run the farm??!!'
'He feels a duty. Even if you don't share it.'
I can smell chicken cooked helplessly on a spit.
Feel nausea in my gorge.
Commotion up ahead.
Suddenly the Turks open the frontier.
'Get your bag,' says my mother. 'We are safe.'
Sack on her shoulder, for the sad, sorry path to
Europe.
I'm rooted to the ground. '…He mustn't fight.
It's suicide.'
'Come on.'
'No. I'm going to stop this nonsense. I'm going to
find Dad.'

The Yazidi's face bursts into light, flared by a match.
He's called Sabah, used to be a cigarette smuggler,
now rescues sex slaves from Raqqa.
'You want to go to Tall Ghazal? To fight?'
'Are you crazy? Want to rescue my father.'
He chuckles.
'What's so funny?'
He draws on his cigarette. 'Get a lot of fathers
asking me to rescue their daughters. Not many
daughters rescuing their fathers.'
'What do you charge?'
'Costs around $10,000 to buy back a slave.'
'WHAT?? I'm not buying anyone, I just want a lift.'
I turn. Ahead, crowds of refugees, and pitiful
cooking fires.
'What have you got?'
I scurry in my bag. Looking for anything.
'…this,' I say sheepishly, producing *Syrian
Family Law*.
'I prefer cash,' he laughs.
'Are you sure? It's a seminal work.'

He opens the boot.

'You can earn your passage.'

Underneath the spare tyre, a compartment, full
of fake ID papers. '"Married couples" attract
less attention.'

Hands me a passport.

'Your name's "Nadia", darling wife.'

The photo's nothing like me: 'This looks like
Mariah Carey.'

'You're much better looking than her.'

(REHANA *rolls her eyes*.)

'Besides, you'll be wearing an abaya.'

Dawn, we drive through a wilderness known only
to the smuggler.

After he's dropped me off, Sabah will go to Mosul.

'Buying a mother and her daughter from their
owner. Quite urgent. Girl's eight. Soon as she
turns nine, they'll take her.'

'Take her?'

'Sell her on. For sex.'

I gasp.

He nods grimly. 'Yeah.'

He shifts uncomfortably. Something in his rear-
view mirror. A nest of smoke and dust. A Land
Cruiser. Horn blazing, lights flashing.

Flying the black-and-white flag of Daesh, like
a skull and crossbones.

We pull over.

The cooling engine ticking like a bomb.

'Don't panic. Remember, you're my wife…
Darling.'

He gets out. Smiling, charming.

Greeting three bearded soldiers. Long guns
pointing vertically, resting on shoulders.

'Peace be with you,' says Sabah.

'Why you driving so fast?' says the leader.

'Dangerous times.'

'Where you going?'

'Farm over the hill.'

The Daesh nods, beckons for papers.

Sabah fumbles in his clothing. The back of his hand,
exposed: covered in ink shapes, crosses and stars.
And suddenly the Daesh's expression changes.
'You are Yazidi?'
'"Was." I converted,' says Sabah, quickly.
'Tattoos are forbidden.'
' – I am a farmer, I cannot afford to remove
them – '
The Daesh nods, thoughtfully. Then leads Sabah
behind the truck –
' – Please, I'm a farmer who – '
A bang. The protesting stops.
One of the Daesh gets in the front, stealing 'wife'
and car.
In the rear window, Sabah's crumpled body.
Shrinking, unburied.
Alone in the desert with vultures.

Pulling into a farm outside Raqqa. A short man
casually walks up and displays his broken,
yellowed teeth.
'What have you got for me, brother?'
'A Yazidi. Found her with her husband,' says
the Daesh.
The Yellow Teeth disappear into a cruel mouth.
'Got too many Yazidis. Pretty?'
'Very.' He shows him the passport. 'Looks like
Mariah Carey.'
'The scientist?'
The Daesh looks blank
'He's thinking of Marie Curie,' I volunteer.
It's as if I haven't spoken.
'She discovered radium. Mariah Carey… Didn't.'
Nothing.
'…a singer?'
I muster my most authoritative, barrister-like
voice, and impose my case for Freedom.
'There's been a mistake. I'm not Yazidi. Was
pretending to be Yazidi, to get to my father. I'm
Muslim.'
Then close my plea by reciting the Shahadah.

I'm in a washroom, in a municipal building in
Raqqa.
Chained to eighteen other women. All under
twenty, young women and girls.
Wrists bleeding and sore, shackles too tight.
My age has conferred responsibility. The younger
girls look to me: but I am thinking only of my
escape.
We're unlocked.
'Get undressed, bathe. And put on the clothes
provided.'
The 'clothes provided' look like dance costumes.
Colourful. Veils and scarves. Warm yellows and
happy pinks. The colours and hues of festivity.
Pretty and alluring. Designed for the male gaze.
This is no dress-up.
Most of the younger kids are obedient, too obedient.
I will be nondescript, invisible. Move slowly.
Choose the dullest, plainest outfit.
'Oi, oi!' One of the guards shouts. 'Get changed.'
Throws a scarf.
It lands messily on my shoulder. I won't flinch,
won't blink.
Suddenly shouts and screams from the bathroom.
Small children squealing.
A cubicle door open.
A blue-eyed girl. Her feet gently twisting in the air.
The sunflower yellow scarf. One end looped
round the mullion of the window. The other round
her neck.
Her face ugly now, discoloured, the fat blue tongue.
Guards arrive, exchange sharp words, juggling the
blame like a hot ember.
I am calm with self-realisation.
I must never take this path.
I must punish them: through guilt. My sole
recourse to a parody of justice.
I turn to the girls. Say with authority.
'Listen. LISTEN. Never be a victim. Look them in
the eyes. Make them see every drop of your pain.

Make them face the consequences of their evil.'
One of the guards grabs me, pushes me into the
corridor.

Then a grand civic room. Soaring marble columns.
Echoing with whoops, baying. Men chittering like
hyenas.
The smell of sweat and moral decay.
I have seen this crowd before: with my father
every Tuesday at the cattle market.
Now I am the livestock. Reduced to my body
parts. Pinched and poked. My fetlocks examined.
Yellow Teeth hustling with a chalkboard price list.
I'm valued at $150. The nine-year-old next to me,
$165.
I will defy. Stare the customers down.
A Sudanese offers a pistol for me.
The trader snorts, 'For her?? She looks like Marie
Carey.'
'Who's Marie Carey?'
'The singer who invented radium.'
'Let me have my share, brother.'
Suddenly, an authoritative voice:
'No one touch her. This woman is for me.'
The crowd parts. I have been selected for rape by
a man of influence.
My owner.
Lupine. Unblinking.
Eyes carrying poison.
Wahid.

Designer furniture, white walls, grey stone floors.
As sterile and functionless as a laboratory.
His flat's not the best in Raqqa: those are allocated
to the foreign fighters, but nevertheless, he must
have influence. Has come a long way since Tall
Ghazal.
How to escape? I have manacles; he has a gun.
He shuts the door. Speaks harshly.
'Take your clothes off.'
'How do you expect me to do that?' I show the
shackles.

He grunts in impatience, produces the key. Begins
to unlock.
Do I butt him, bite him?
He senses my intent, 'Your crazy father isn't here
to protect you now, little farm girl. Your life is
over. Submit.'
Never, never.
'Would you treat your mother or sisters like this?'
'You are my ghanimah, my Spoils of War.'
'My body is your reward??'
'It is permitted.'
He puts the gun down, to undress.
I need time.
'I need the toilet.'
'Be out in two minutes, or I'll kick the door down.'
The manacles fall to the floor.

I lock the toilet door.
Two minutes.
I'm a cornered animal. Eyes goggling. Looking
for a weapon, something, anything. I must find
claws. Fangs.
A toilet brush? – no weapon of war.
I take the lid off the cistern.
A low hissing.
The ballcock, on a metal rod.
The rod…?? Could be a spear, a skewer?
I try and rip it off.
It bends.
The water hisses, threatening.
'What's going on in there?'
I pull again. The rod's torn, but doesn't come free.
Strain opens the wounds on my wrists.
Drips of blood in the cistern. Expanding like dark
jellyfish.
My blood. My last line of defence.
'Come on, come on.'
I pull down my underwear, squeeze my bleeding
wrist, let the drops fall.
THUMP. The door thuds and trembles.
Cracks and splinters round the hinge.

THUMP. He's body-charging.

I pull my clothes on.

The door snaps open. His talons find my hair.

He grabs me, drags me, throws me spinning onto the sofa.

No longer wearing trousers. A vile earthworm of flesh.

He pounces, a forearm across my throat.

I claw at his eyes. But my abaya's betraying me, riding up.

Suddenly he stops. Pulls up. Points between my legs.

'You're bleeding.

'Yes, I'm bleeding. It's my period.'

He stands in horror.

'It is forbidden to…!'

His rifle's unguarded against the wall.

'Put your clothes on,' he shrieks, authority draining from his voice, like blood from his shrinking organ.

I stand.

He steps back.

I jeer, 'Come on. Fuck me. Fuck me and be damned.'

I advance, he retreats.

Now, now. I'm close enough.

Snatch the gun.

'You don't know how to use that.'

I release the safety catch, with a confident click.

'Oh, but I do.'

He turns white.

I am not able to kill.

But life-on-the-farm has taught me how to tie knots.

I leave him gagged and trussed up like a chicken.

He will not be found before morning.

I hurry into the street, elated, terrified.

Mercifully, there are no street lights; a curfew.

Darkness my friend.

Groping, fumbling, stumbling through the streets for an age.

Escaping: I don't know where.

Away.

Free, free.

For how long?

Suddenly my hand brushes Hell.

I yelp loud.

I touched a crucified body.

I'm in a square, where there are dozens of them, hung up for all. Signs round their necks itemising their violations of the law.

I feel the touch of the corpse like a branding.

And wipe and wipe.

Too preoccupied to hear the sound of the engine.

Suddenly, I'm pinned in the headlights.

I panic, turn, run, fall into a fermenting mountain of bin sacks.

I try to push up, flailing like a beetle.

The truck stops with a whistle. A Daesh pennant on the front.

The driver steps in front of the headlights.

With a shotgun.

'Where is your husband? You should be escorted, sister.'

He is backlit, glowing like the Divine.

'Help me, help me. If they find me, they'll kill me. I'm looking for my father.'

He's an oil trader. Permitted to drive any time of day or night: Daesh need oil more than a curfew.

He will release me at the oilfields, near the border.

But I can't sit on the passenger seat. I might be seen.

He lowers the backrest, must squeeze into the space behind.

'If they find you, I don't know how you got here, right? You sneaked in when I was parked, yeah?'

'Why are you helping me?'

'I have a daughter, too.'

'You're Daesh?'

'Kurdish.'

'...You fly the Daesh flag?' I say of the pennant.

He scurries in the glovebox. Produces a YPG flag.

'Depends where I'm driving. A trader does what
he has to.'
'You serve two masters?'
'Daesh–YPG – it's all the same.'
'Not to women it isn't.'
'I'm a trader. Traders follow the money.'
I laugh bitterly. The verdict of laughter stings him.
'What do you expect me to do? What can one
person do?' He says miserably.
There's silence. Just the growls of the truck.
'I'm helping you, aren't I?' He protests. 'What are
you doing to stop them?'
I shift uncomfortably, my damp abaya protesting
on the screeching vinyl.

Sunrise, in a village East of Kobani: the metallic
swipe of a missile. It screeches past the
windscreen. Slams into the road, punching us with
a giant fist of flame.
Suddenly.
The oilman screaming, the tanker on two wheels.
Sliding sideways, screeching rubber.
I'm tossed into the air.
As we judder to a halt in cornfields.
'RUN! RUN!' screams the oilman, already
leaping into the corn. Sprinting for the safety of
a farmhouse.
Distant shouts and rattles.
'RUN before it blows up!!'
Squeeze out. In the fields. Running. Breathless.
Crackles of gunfire.
Bullets whip the crop.
The farmhouse ahead. Some kind of shelter.
Shouts behind, they're chasing.
Dive behind the farmhouse wall.
'You okay?' he says.
Bullets hitting the wall. Zip zip.
Shouts, closer.
A bullet nicks the corner, am sprayed with masonry.
'Surrender.' Our only option.
'We have no white flag.'

'Use the pennants.'

'Daesh or YPG?'

'Pick one, the right one, the wrong one, we're dead.'

The oilman gambles.

Steps out.

'Ho!' Whistles. Waves the Daesh flag.

The shooting stops.

It works. He smiles.

Suddenly his chest explodes.

They're YPG.

Zip. Zip.

Any second I'll be shot. By my own side.

I step out. Arms in the air. Singing till I'm hoarse.

'Comrades unite, for we will be free, Come shed your blood for Kurdistan.'

They rise from the corn. Guns still pointing. A unit of six women.

Buttresses of earth protecting an old primary school.

Flying a bright-yellow flag with a bright-red star.

The children long gone. In the playground, women at drill.

I'm led down a cool corridor. Photos on the walls.

Colourful headshots, like pictures of the staff.

I recognise one of the women, a farmer's wife.

'It's Gamesh! I know her!'

My captors don't reply.

'Who are these?'

'The martyrs. We bear their photos, to remember them.'

On a porch, the Commander.

Small, about thirty. Handsome and lethal.

'So. You are the girl who waves the flag of Daesh – whilst singing the songs of Liberation. What are you? Friend or Foe?'

'Friend, friend, I'm trying to find my father, he's defending Tall Ghazal.'

'Won't be now. The Resistance withdrew to Kobane.'

She walks to the balustrade, looks out over the
playground. 'So your father's a Hero. And will
you fight for your country, too?'
'I'm a pacifist,' I laugh, unsure.
She snorts. 'You might not want to fight Daesh,
but Daesh are fighting you. You're everything they
hate: Western, Liberal, Educated.'
She watches a buzzard circle the fields.
'...You asked about Gamesh. They captured her;
tied her hair to a car bumper. Drove. When they'd
finished with her, there was nothing left below the
breast bone.'
A rabbit jinks in the buzzard's sights.
'If you don't fight them, that's the system of
justice which will prevail. If you don't fight, you
facilitate; if you facilitate, you collaborate.'
The raptor swoops, talons forwards.
'Your only choice is between two sets of violence.
One that empowers you, one which enslaves you.'
Silence.
The buzzard in the field, pulling strings of meat
with a sharp beak.

I dine with the recruits. They too are shameless
carnivores, smacking lips, tearing meat from bone.
Suddenly, an officer exclaims,
'Rehana?'
A girl called Lubena, from Tall Gahzal.
After days of hostility, a friendly face. I hug her
with tears.
'I heard about Gamesh.'
She squats by me, plucks some rice from a bowl.
'She broke the golden rule. She forgot to "save the
last bullet for herself".'
'These people! Don't they scare you?'
'We scare them. They have been told that if they
are killed by a woman, they cannot enter Paradise.
No seventy-two virgins for them.'
'Is that true?'
'That's what they say.'
She rolls the rice into a ball.

'So you coming to join us?'

'I'm more use in a court of law, than a theatre of war,' I smile.

Says quietly, 'I doubt it. I know all about your father's "training exercises"…'

I'm baffled.

'He used to buy Orangina from my father's shop.'

She pops the ball in her mouth. Like a giant full stop.

The dishes cleared, she stands, calls for attention.

'Okay, comrades, post-dinner treat: we're going to play a game. The winner gets the pick of the mattresses.'

By the response, it's a good prize.

'Who Can Clean a Rifle – Blindfold.'

Guffaws and gasps. Cries of 'impossible'.

She lays her rifle between us.

It's a Dragunov. Like my father's. Lubena throws me a pointed glance.

Then instructs a large peasant girl to go first.

A poor effort, fumbling fingers, giggles of embarrassment and dropped bolts.

Big smiles. Embarrassed giggles all round. 'It's impossible.'

I smirk, superior.

Lubena smiles. 'Perhaps our guest should go next.'

She thrusts the blindfold.

Oh. Oh.

Impossible to decline.

I wear the blindfold, the gun in my hands.

Easy. I flow:

Prepare ramrod. Flannelette, solvent.

Rifle: Safety off. Magazine off. Action back.

Move to front. Ramrod in, push-slide, push-slide. Ramrod down.

Move behind. Wipe the chamber. Action forward.

Magazine – on. Safety – on.

Done.

I take the blindfold off, see respect in a circle.

And the Commander nodding in the doorway.

'You teach my recruits how to do that, I promise
you, if your father's alive, I will find him.'

Kobane. A cloudless dawn, after an airless night.
It will be a hot day.
We're in a forward base, a destroyed apartment
block in street 48.
My father's wounded. In an improvised hospital,
downtown. I will be taken to see him this
afternoon, if I'm not killed first.
The shelling started after dawn prayer.
Insistent pecking machine guns. Explosions, funnels
of smoke. The fighting: close, getting closer.
Lubena laughs, 'Hey, if I get killed, you can have
my iPod.'
'Fuck THAT!' I snort. 'It's got Justin Bieber on it.'
Ten o'clock.
The surprising roar of an engine. A car at the top
of the road, juddering over fallen masonry and
debris. Engine straining hard.
'Stop, whoa whoa, ho! Slow down!'
But the engine becomes higher pitched. It's
speeding up.
A hundred yards away, ninety...
Suddenly everybody starts shooting at it.
...seventy, sixty...
The windscreen shatters, the driver flails.
...fifty...
Suddenly. The car detonates. Day: instantly night.
A car door. Hundreds of feet in the sky.
Folds of cloud.
Ears ringing, commotion. A shower of
plasterwork.
Struggling to breathe, gasping hot air.
Noises, indistinct.
I push myself up. A Daesh seeping through the
smoke.
Dark clothes, dark beard.
Allah Akhbar.
Bang. Lubena drops him, shoots another.

Wave after wave. Born of the black cloud.
'Come on, Rehana, shoot shoot, grab a gun,
come on.'
She shoots shoots shoots.
The zip of bullets in the room.
Am crouching. Screaming. Arms over head.
A yelp. Suddenly Lubena. Clutching her eye.
Tendrils of blood on her concrete-powdered face.
Blinks blinks, 'Can't see, can't see.'
Thrusts the Dragunov. 'Take it. Shoot, SHOOT.'
The street beneath. Dozens of Daesh.
Flitting from doorway to doorway. A block away.
We're going to die.
'Take it.'
And I feel eyes on me.
TAKE IT.
Am seen by a Daesh, in the street.
TAKEITTAKEITTAKEIT.
And suddenly I'm twelve years old, and my father
is holding out the Dragunov – SHOOT HIM – and
my tears are flowing – SHOOT! – and I'm in the
Daesh sights – SHOOT! – SHOOT THE DOG
SHOOT THE DOG – his finger is on the trigger –
SHOOT. THE. DOG.

A reflex, a sudden twitch of the finger.
The hole in his chest small.
He spirals. Falls.
I see the exit wound.
A dinner plate of flesh missing from his back.
I have killed. I am a killer.

Suddenly it's easy.

Loading and shooting and loading and the
Orangina tins are falling over and over and I have
killed and I am a killer again and again.

…And with every kill, a small death of my own.
Each bullet ricocheting into my gasping core.
Compassion bleeding pale.
In the court of Rehana, there are no mitigating
circumstances. There is only one verdict: Death…

The rapist with his nine-year-old sex slave? –
Death.
The religious bigot who'd kill all gays – Death.
The homesick boy who made a terrible mistake? –
Death.
The shy boy who only followed his brother –
Death…

…The farmer's daughter who was a Pacifist? –
Death.

Death.

…The cemetery is in Daesh territory.
We bury our own in a school playground.
Our graves, next to a weathered slide and an
inappropriately garish roundabout.
Lubena's final resting place. A breeze block her
tombstone.
I weep and weep.
Less for her death, more for my own.
I have killed I am a killer.
Like an epitaph in the lost innocence of the
playground.

A roundabout turns in the wind.

I'm in an improvised hospital ward in the surgery
of a vet.
Where is he? Where's my father?
'Angel!'
On a cot at the back, his shrunken figure.
He smiles, the strength of his smile isn't matched
in his arms.
Can't even sit upright.
'How you feeling?'
He chuckles, 'If I was one of the animals they'd
have put me down.'
(*A look of concern from* REHANA.)
'You become William Shatner yet?'
'No, but I briefly became Mariah Carey.'
'The woman who discovered radium?'
'Something like that.'
He coughs, each heave bringing agony.

(REHANA *struggles to say something… a painful
confession. Then:*)
'I've become a killer, Dad. I have become
a monster. I have lost myself.'
He smiles, weakly pats my fingers, looks to the
skylight, watching the glide of the rapidly
moving clouds.
Then says, 'I was only in the mountains for six
months, but then my father died, and I was sucked
in the farm. The pull of the ancestors, too strong…
Aye aye aye. I should have finished my fight.
Bequeathed you a land fit for your law.'
'Don't blame YOURself!'
'No. If you are truly committed to justice… you
will have to seize it. Wade through blood to snatch
it from the barbarians. It's the dread paradox. That
to create a land free from tyranny, we must be as
bloody as the tyrants themselves.'
My shoulders shaking.
'…Wipe your tears. Death happens.'
Always, the farmer's pragmatic attitude to life
and death.
My colleagues cough from the doorway.
'I'm sorry I couldn't save you, Dad.'
'But you did. I live on, in you.'
Our last kiss.
As I link arms with my two YPJ colleagues, his
song escorts us into the street.
'All the single ladies, all the single ladies…'

I'm at one with the ruins of the town.
Crumbled like the neat, considered streets.
Wearing its dust and powder like camouflage.
Invisible amongst the stones. Controlling my
breathing. Ignoring every itch. Motionless like the
crocodile, waiting to strike.
And when the unsuspecting Daesh raises an
unguarded head:
Squeeze.
He joins me in death.
And I feel nothing.

Pistachios on the trees look like olives with pretty
velvet skins, yellows, greens, and blushing purple.
But pinch the fruits, and the thin jacket slides away.
Not a fruit at all, no soft flesh. Just a hard stone.

We are content and weary, driving back from the
front in the late afternoon sun. Our bullets all
fired, our muscles spent.
After six months of fighting, we're pushing back
the enemy, sweeping the villages.
Clearing booby-trapped toys, disarming tripwires.
I have claimed my hundredth victim.
Suddenly we are in all-too-familiar terrain.
A silhouette I recognise and love. The farmhouses,
the little mosque. Tall Ghazal.
'Whoa, ho!'
I bang on the roof of the pick-up. 'Stop, stop! Can
we just…?'

We pull into the farmyard of my youth.
The house, lifeless. The interiors dark and
foreboding. Graffiti on the walls. Excrement on
the floor. My textbooks gone.

My young comrades have never seen me cry
before. To them I am the Angel, the emotionless
killer. My tears are unsettling, unnerving.
Alarmed and respectful, they stay back.

As I walk to the trees.
Their trees, his trees, my trees.
Our trees.

There are no birds, no song. Just an eerie
sepulchral silence.
The lines of trees like tombstones. Burnt, all burnt.
Benny's tree – the grandest of them all – a huge
black skeleton, like a giant fossil.
The work of my father, my grandfather. His father
before him. Charcoal. Gone. Never to have
existed.
And now, with the death of the trees, now, right
now, this is when my father dies.

– and my fingers are clawing the sky like Benny's agonised, twisted branches.

This is the harvest, this is their harvest. A charred black nothing.

I return via the outhouses.
The rusting tools untouched. A wince at the sight of my father's machete.
The names of Isis fighters charcoaled on the walls.
Epitaphs for dead martyrs.
A pile of ash, a spent campfire.
I find my legal textbooks. All charred. They've been used for fuel.
Fire still warm.
Oh no.
Mattresses...
A base... they're using our outhouse as a base.

Suddenly – voices. Men's voices.
Coming my way.
A glimpse of black bandanas, heavy dark weaponry.
Nowhere to run. Only one entrance.
My magazine is spent. I have no ammo.
Frantic.
Find the cylinder of metal at my breast. The last bullet.
Fumbling fingers pull back the bolt.
My hundred and first victim: Myself.
Barrel in my mouth.
A shriek of alarm, from the Daesh at the door.
Seven men.
Frozen.
My finger resting on the trigger.
Then I see him.
The Daesh guide with the local knowledge.
Wahid.
Everything in slow motion.
The crick of their weaponry as they begin to react.

I put it to the jury that he cannot be master of my corpse.

– that he cannot go to Paradise.
– that he cannot rape the seventy-two virgins in
the afterworld.
– that he.
– must die at a woman's hand.

The barrel out of my mouth.
Levelling the cross-sight between his legs.
He screams.
Guilty.
Squeeze.
An ejaculate of blood.

The Best Justice I can muster.

And now the pack are all over me. Each holding
an arm, a leg, pinning my shoulders.
One lifts the machete from the shelf, pulls my
hair, exposing my neck.
Touches the blade on my throat, lining up a final
blow.

This is how it ends.

And as he raises my father's machete, I begin
laughing, thinking: You can't kill me. Even when
you tear my head from its body. Because I have
been killed a long time ago.
But will be reborn here.
My blood in the soil, feeding every crop. Every tree.
An everlasting farmer, a Ghazali.
The farmer's daughter.
The father's daughter.
The fruit-bearing tree.

Beam me up, Scotty.

10 Questions I Always Get Asked About The *Arabian Nightmares*
Henry Naylor

Where does your obsession with the Middle East stem from?

I've been a topical, satirical writer for the past twenty-odd years – a period which has encompassed 9/11, the War on Terror, the rise of IS and Islamic fundamentalism. The biggest stories of the age have all stemmed from the region. To write viable satire in the period, you had to have a handle on the issues. I've read thousands of articles on the subject.

But there was a specific incident which particularly piqued my interest, during the War on the Taliban in 2001.

It was the moment I saw a BBC reporter being blown up live on air.

William Reeve was the journalist – an old-school BBC man, broadcasting from a makeshift studio in downtown Kabul – as the Allies were launching their final assaults on the city.

He was talking about how the bombing was getting closer and closer – when suddenly – live on air – the wall of the studio blew up, blasting him – mercifully unhurt – off his chair.

The cameraman yelled 'Jesus Christ!' and ran in front of the camera –

– and I nearly fell off my own chair: not because of William Reeve's misfortune, but because the cameraman was my lovely old flatmate, Phil Goodwin.

I was already beginning to form the idea for a play about the experiences of war correspondents (which was to become *Finding Bin Laden*) – and after the war, I phoned up Phil, and tried to pick his brains for research. By the end of the call, he'd persuaded me to go to Kabul in Afghanistan.

So after having plundered Phil's contacts list (!) I travelled with a director-friend, Sam Maynard, to Kabul. We spent several days checking out the damage, and speaking to war victims. We went round refugee camps, we even went to Bagram Airbase.

The trip completely changed my life. Up until that point I had been a satirical writer sat at my desk at home sneering about events on the news.

Actually immersing myself in a news event first-hand transformed my writing. It gradually became harder to 'be funny'. It became more important to tell the Truth of War Victims' stories.

You used to be a comedian. Why did you suddenly start writing 'serious' plays?

When I started writing *The Collector* – I thought I *was* going to write a comedy. Albeit a dark one.

But the more work I did on it, the more I realised I had some serious points I wanted to make – which I didn't want to undermine by overloading the piece with comedy.

I also think I was getting a bit bored of writing satirical sketches. I'd been doing it constantly for about twenty years. And was not stretching myself. I could kind of do it on auto-pilot. The same news stories kept cropping up every time we got a new government. Effectively, I was writing the same sketches over and over. A sketch written in 1980s, say, about the Tories screwing up the Health Service could be used again in 2017, if you just swapped Ken Clarke's name for Jeremy Hunt.

Don't you miss performing?

My hair's falling out. I've got a few wrinkles. I don't think an audience would want to look at me for long.

Seriously, I'm reluctant to 'write for myself'. I find that, when I'm writing for myself, I ask myself the wrong questions. I start asking myself questions like: 'What would I like to do on stage?' rather than – 'What does the *character* need to do on stage?' It's a mistake. The story and the character's truth have to come first.

Some performers can do it. I can't. At least at the moment.

Was the switch from comedy to drama difficult?

At the premiere of *The Collector*, I was absolutely terrified. I had no idea if it was any good. Waiting for the reviews was nerve-racking. But I think it's important to scare yourself like that. If you're scared – you're clearly doing something different as an artist. And the fear makes you raise your game, for fear of looking an idiot.

Why did you call the play The Collector?

A fair question.

To be honest, due to Edinburgh Fringe brochure deadlines – I had to come up with a title before I wrote the play.

I'm rather embarrassed to say that, when I named my play *The Collector* – I'd never heard of John Fowles' classic of the same name.

At the time, I thought the show was going to be about an Abu Ghraib prison guard who 'collected', and sold, creepy war memorabilia from his 'tour' in Iraq.

But once I started writing the show, the Collector became a different person altogether. She became Zoya – a young, female Collector of music.

If I was to rename it, now, I'd call it *Collaborators*.

But, hey.

I was surprised that Echoes *was written by a man...?*

I think it's an indictment of our industry that people have to ask that question. It shows not enough good parts *are* being written for women.

I think there's an awful lot of navel-gazing on the part of many male playwrights, who can't/won't look beyond their own sex!

Personally, I enjoy writing for women. I'm proud of the fact that five of the six roles in this collection are female.

I find it easy to empathise with characters with a feminist perspective as, in my day-to-day life, I'm surrounded by strong, intelligent women. I also feel that in the Middle East the female story is largely untold.

How much of The Angel's story is true?

Frankly, not much is known about her.

Yes, there was a person called Rehana. She was a law student who jettisoned her studies to fight for the Kobane resistance. But that's about all the facts we *know*.

And beyond that – accounts differ. Some people say she was a prolific sniper who shot a hundred jihadis. Others say that number is vastly exaggerated.

She's become an internet myth.

People don't even know whether she's alive or dead.

Jihadis have posted pictures online of a grinning soldier holding up the severed head of a woman who they claim is Rehana.

The Kurds have responded, by posting a picture of Rehana looking alive and well – and flipping a V sign at the camera.

One of them is wrong!

Does it bother you that you might not be historically accurate?

The fact is, the show's a drama, not a history essay. As a dramatist, my duty is to write a story which is entertaining and moving. To create my own truth and stick with it.

And I believe I've done it convincingly. I've intensively researched life in the Kobane region. It's a very agricultural area, and so I've made 'my' Rehana a pistachio farmer's daughter. After all my research – I've become a bit of a pistachio-growing expert, I reckon!

What links the three plays?

Thematically, there are strong feminist undertones.

And in each, young people try to discover their identity.

The stories are large and vast: epics, which are more akin to movies than theatre shows. The distance covered by the protagonists – both physically and emotionally – is huge.

In terms of presentation, all the characters pierce the 'fourth wall' with their monologues.

Your plays are all very minimal in their staging; there are never any sets. How did you arrive at that style?

The plays all premiered at the Gilded Balloon at the Edinburgh Festival. They were written for a fringe format. As a result, a certain style had to be adopted...

In Edinburgh there are often eight shows on in the venue. Fifteen minutes between each performance. Seven-and-a-half minutes to erect the set, and get the audience in; seven-and-a-half to take it down, and get them out.

Circumstance forces you to be minimalist. There isn't time to set up an elaborate or intricate set.

So we used a backcloth and three chairs in the premiere of *The Collector*. A bench and a stool in *Echoes*.

And by the time we made *Angel*, director Michael Cabot reduced the set to just a barrel.

Personally, I enjoy the challenge of having no set. It places more emphasis on the writing, the acting and the directing. There's nowhere to hide. You've got to be on top of your game.

It forces the writer to go deeper into his or her characters.

Now you've completed the trilogy – what next?

It's funny you know. I never set out to write a trilogy.

But the Middle Eastern story keeps evolving and changing so fast – that I keep finding something new I want to say.

So the truth is, I might write a fourth instalment, *if* a great story leaps out at me. Or even a fifth. Could even do a George Lucas and do seven parts!

www.nickhernbooks.co.uk

facebook.com/nickhernbooks

twitter.com/nickhernbooks